Finding Your
Internship

What Employers Want You To Know

The Most Important Book Students And Their Parents Will Ever Read

Marvin A. Russell

Marvin A. Russell

Finding Your **Internship**

Also by Marvin A. Russell

Linebacker in the Boardroom: Lessons in Life and Leadership

Marv Russell's Blog: http//www.marvrussell.com/blog

@TheInternZone

@marvrussell

@ndlinebacker

http://www.facebook.com/FindYourInternImpactZone

Finding Your Internship: What Employers Want You To Know
Marvin A. Russell

Front and Back cover design:	Marvin C. Russell
Chief Copyeditor:	Mary Ann Falkenberg
Chief Content Editor:	Catherine M. Russell
Content Editor:	Kristen J. Talbot
Case Study Contribution:	Drew Tilson
Case Study Contribution:	Marty Falkenberg
Case Study Contribution:	Brian Falkenberg
Case Study Contribution:	Rachel Wilhelm
Case Study Contribution:	Bonnie Kaye
Case Study Contribution:	Mike Andrito
Case Study Contribution:	Mike Kaye

First published by Dog Ear Publishing
4010 W. 86th Street, Ste H
Indianapolis, IN 46268
www.dogearpublishing.net

ISBN: 978-1-4575-2010-5

This book is printed on acid-free paper.

Printed in the United States of America

Dedication

This book is dedicated to Mary Falkenberg-Igaravidez and John Moriarty, my sister-in-law and brother-in-law who we recently lost. Loving and enthusiastic parents of bright young students, Mary and John enriched our family with their humor and love. Our fond memories of them soothe the pain of their loss. We will always remember stories and good times...

The Outlaws

Mani-Pedis

Pool Parties

Tacky Blowup Christmas Decorations

The Backyard Owls

The Lady Cave

Neighborhood Garage Parties

Christmas Eve Family Celebrations

Outstanding leaders enable us to learn, and they inspire us to become more than we dreamed we could be. They engage, empower, motivate and inspire others to reach their potential, realize their dreams and create an impact on the world around them. An internship is a first step toward realizing your leadership potential. Use it as an opportunity to learn and shape your career as a leader.

—Marv Russell

Table of Contents

FORWARD
By Abby Kohut

I have been a recruitment executive and consultant for over 15-years and have hired or managed the hiring of 10,000+ people. I have seen everything and I have heard everything. I have seen what to do and certainly, what not to do to be successful. But, when I heard Marv's approach to finding an internship for the first time, I realized immediately the brilliance of his process, ideas and advice to interns.

I have long been a supporter of internships. In fact, the University of Rochester encouraged me to participate in a variety of internships while I was an undergraduate. My internships helped me develop teamwork, character, time management skills, dependability and responsibility. I also learned about the world of work and how to get along with different people that had varying opinions. Best of all, I learned what I liked to do and what I didn't like to do – what a HUGE gift that was at such a young age!

As I progressed in the Human Resources function, I designed internship programs and hired many interns within them. Many of those interns went on to fulfilling careers in the areas that they tested. Others chose to pursue other dreams. All of them found great value in their internship.

Marv's approach to finding an internship is brilliantly simple and it mirrors the teachings that I provide to jobseekers at later stages of their careers as I travel across the country. Don't follow the crowd… do things differently. Use your skills to market yourself and to explain why you are better than your peers. Think outside the box and you will succeed beyond your wildest dreams.

I have worked with Marv for years, but more importantly, he is my friend. I am honored to have been asked to write this forward.

Abby Kohut, who is known by recruiting professionals, job seekers, clients and across the web as **Absolutely Abby**, is the President of Staffing Symphony, LLC. In the past 16 years, Abby has held recruitment leadership positions with Kaplan, Continuum Health Partners and Alpharma. Her website **www.AbsolutelyAbby.com** and her books "Absolutely Abby's 101 Job Search Secrets" and "Absolutely Abby's Top 12 Interview Questions Exposed" teach candidates tools, techniques and the secrets of the job search process that other recruiters won't tell you. Abby has been seen providing job search tips on Fox 5 Business News, ABC's Good Morning Connecticut, The Joe Franklin Show on

Bloomberg Radio and as a keynote speaker in numerous seminars, forums and expos. Abby was selected as one of "The Monster 11 for 2011: Career Experts Who Can Help Your Job Search" and is one of the "Top 100 Influential People Online" according to Fast Company Magazine. Since 2010, Abby has been on a mission to help one million job seekers overcome difficulties of the job search process. In her 2012-13 nationwide tour of America, Abby continues her mission, journey and effort to achieve her million-jobseeker goal – to connect with and assist a million jobseekers fulfill their career goals. Learn more about Abby's programs, seminars, tools and her tour of America at **www.AbbyAcrossAmerica.com**

From the desk of the SVP Human Resources

Career development has become a complicated process of our professional life in the 21st Century. For Millennials this decade has demanded creativity, perseverance, and willingness to own and guide your own career. Facing difficult economic conditions the Millennials are faced with a lack of first time job opportunities as they graduate from universities across the United States. Securing internships has become an art form and the techniques to achieve success have become a science in terms of the processes, procedures and methodologies at your disposal.

This book, *Finding Your Internship: What Employers Want You To Know,* was written as a roadmap to internship achievement. The tools and techniques offered have been designed and offered in a simple format enabling readers to create opportunities for immediate internship success. More importantly, ***the tools and advice given in this book come from the perspective and voice of companies that hire these interns each day.*** Companies try to live with and try to understand academic and governmental rules and regulations and often what is considered non-valued-added bureaucracy. Companies believe in the internships. But they also believe your success as an intern begins with your ownership of a search process, your desire to achieve career goals you have set for yourself and willingness to listen to a voice coming from the corporate perspective. Finding your ideal internship is a lengthy process, demanding hard work and follow up. It demands that you understand that you will most likely have frustration before you achieve ultimate success. However, your ultimate success in finding the ideal internship will be a rewarding experience.

Marv Russell

Author

Acknowledgements

Thanks to the Queen Mum, Mary Ann Falkenberg, my mother-in-law who has been a tremendous supporter of my work as an author and speaker. Her skills as Chief Copyeditor of this book have been greatly appreciated.

Thanks to Theresa Laurenzo and Jodi Plett of **Elite EA's Inc.** for your support, patience and assistance as Marv Russell and Partners has grown and matured as a company. **Elite EA's Inc.** provides unparalleled administrative support to me and to other professionals across South Florida

Thanks to Abby Kohut "Absolutely Abby" and her husband, Ken Kohut, for their friendship, partnership, ideas and collaboration.

Thanks to Kristen Talbot for your contributions to this book, especially serving as an editor, representing the target population of *Finding Your Internship*. Best wishes as you enter your senior year of college. Continue to Find Your Impact Zone, The Place Where You Make the Difference in the World Around You.

Thanks to Brian Falkenberg, Mike Andrito, Marty Falkenberg, Mike Kaye, Rachel Wilhelm and Drew Tilson for your contributions and representing the target population of this book.

Thanks to Vince and my friends, especially Don, Dr. Tom, Scott, Ira, Patrick, Mike and Anthony at the **Smoke Inn Cigar Bar in Delray Beach, FL.**, for your support, friendship, a place to write this book and for protecting my favorite seat.

Special thanks to Dr. Tom Clark, a dear friend, advisor, mentor and supporter of my work.

INTRODUCTION

AN INTERNSHIP IS A JOB: You Want It... Be Prepared... Be Aggressive and Go Get It!!!

Let's get it straight: An internship is a job, it's not a nice thing to do, it's not an optional thing to do...It's a must thing to do to jump-start your career. However, if you want it you have to be prepared, be aggressive and make it happen.

I have coached, counseled and taught hundreds of individuals how to find the right internship or the right job. The key – Don't sit around and wait for a job to come to you. You have to MAKE the opportunity and create the ideal proposal that a prospective employer feels warrants hiring you.

Today everyone is searching for an internship, co-op, practicum or fellowship to:

- Gain valuable job experience

- Fulfill course requirements for academic credit

- Test-drive career options

- Prepare for grad school opportunity

- Hopefully make a little money, or

- Possibly lead to being hired into a full-time job

Getting an internship is smart and necessary, but first you must find or create internship opportunities. Many students and parents believe that internship opportunities are few and far between and that they all belong to people with connections: I don't agree!

> *Internship opportunities are everywhere but they come in different places, shapes and forms. You can't limit your options in your search. You must use all the sources at your disposal and create new sources.*

Is it easy – no - it's hard work but it will be a rewarding effort, not IF, but WHEN you land the job. My objective in this book is to teach you to make your own internship opportunities – to mold and shape every relationship that you and your parents, friends and relatives have at your disposal and develop it into a potential opportunity. The fact is you need to start looking at internships no differently than searching for that first job.

This book is not long and it's not complex. I go directly to the point with my formula, tools and techniques for internship success. I have 3 objectives to Find Your Intern Impact Zone.

1. The search for the right internship is no different than searching for a regular job – it takes time, research, the right process and follow-through.

2. The best internship is the one that you have tailored to your personal and professional needs.

3. When performed in the proper framework, an internship has greater value than a regular summer paying job that has no relationship to your career goals and education.

I spent over 30-years in Human Resources, and worked my way up from recruiter on the factory floor to a HR Generalist to Senior VP of HR for multinational corporations, in a variety of industries including manufacturing, pharmaceuticals and healthcare. I've worked in non-profit, government, and for profit. I've served on boards. I worked overseas as an ex-pat for nearly 10 years, and taught in the MBA program of *HEC (Haute Ecole Commericale),* Paris, France's prestigious business school and source of a great majority of CEOs of French companies. I have personally hired thousands of employees and supervised the hiring of tens of thousands more in all these corporations; in every single place I've worked, every field, every country, I've hired interns and ***seldom were these internships publicized.***

For years, students, family, friends and colleagues have asked me to assist in finding an internship, a first job, and for career advice. In some cases, I was able to personally hire those interns. Other times I made referrals that resulted in internships. But always I was able to provide advice, counsel, resources, recommendations and tips that gave the student information and practical steps that made their internship search more likely to result in getting an internship.

My advice is tough and realistic and yes, I challenge the career development departments of universities, and some students and parents don't like that. OK, I get it – you're spending lots of money for that education so they must know what they are talking about.

Universities, parents, friends and godparents and aunts and uncles do have a lot of good advice, but the world changes constantly and I have one simple comparison. I've hired thousands of interns and employees in large and small companies. How many people has the school's career counselor hired lately? I don't want to be rude or cruel, but *you need to listen to the lessons of experience in this tough job market you face and not limit your options.*

AN INTERNSHIP IS A JOB: ACT LIKE IT

I want to be clear. An internship is a job. It may not pay money. It may be crappy work. It may be boring. Nevertheless, it is a job and not having an internship or not doing an internship will cost you in terms of starting your career.

Let's also admit that many people in companies or business view an internship as a challenge in our difficult marketplace. You are considered an individual with limited or no experience, who may have to be baby-sat, who will have little if no initiative and someone who will be dumped on another low-level person in the organization who is probably overworked and underpaid. This person may view you as a threat to their job. Your job as an intern is to learn, contribute to the success of the organization and give your best effort. When you do this you will be received as a value-added asset and welcome addition to the team.

My job is to assist you in proving the stereotypes of internships to be false and assist you in finding your Internship Impact Zone – the place where you and your gifts and talents can be molded, shaped and developed into a package that is respected and provides an immediate contribution to impact those around you, so you are viewed as someone who has potential to provide a long-term substantive contribution that can result in various forms of compensation, solid references and future opportunities.

This book should help you understand why the attainment of an internship and the successful completion of your internship are so important:

- During economic downturns, internships become a viable method to achieve basic skills

- Those individuals with proven job skills will have an advantage for full-time permanent positions

- Internships assist in developing confidence and self-assurance in one's capabilities

- Internships demonstrate your initiative and desire to learn, often at a younger age than permanent employees

- The search for an internship is the precursor to the search for a full-time, permanent job

- Internships in your high school years can be a factor in getting into the college of your choice by demonstrating your commitment to community service, hard work, multi-tasking and your commitment to personal and professional development

- Internships in your college years can be a factor in getting the job of your choice by demonstrating your hard work, multi-tasking and success orientation

Internships can be structured in a variety of perspectives and contexts. The terms *internship, co-ops, practicums or fellowships* are used to describe opportunities used by business, healthcare, government and not-for-profit environments to provide learning opportunities on-the-job. Internships are normally shorter in duration and co-ops often are as long as 6 months. The term fellowship is most often used in clinical environments and can be a year plus in length. In this book I have used the word *internship* as generic term to define these experiential learning opportunities. These experiences come in a number of forms and context; however, each are designed around learning and refining knowledge, skills, abilities and reinforcing and refining your academic framework. There are multiple ways that these internships are structured and setup in terms of the value provided to the intern. Each context is not mutually exclusive of the other:

- Attain academic credit only

- Attain professional experience only

- Attain academic credit and receive monetary remuneration or other benefits

This book contains 20 steps or what I call **"20 Intern Impact Zones"** that create a path to successfully securing the right internship opportunity. Each step is focused on you and your efforts, behaviors and willingness to commit to the process. If you want an internship, then you have to own and manage the process and stop whining and telling everyone that all the good jobs are gone, or that you couldn't interview when the companies were on campus because your counselor screwed up.

At the end of each Impact Zone chapter I offer pieces of the advice *From the desk of the SVP Human Resources*. These pieces of advice summarize the most important points I have made in each chapter. You will also find *Available Online Resources* that will provide you articles regarding the various elements of the chapter. Use these resources to supplement the information that I have provided in this book.

Ladies and gentlemen, it's time to grow up and stop making excuses and make things happen. If you end the school year and have no options on the table, you are doing something fundamentally wrong and have not put forth sufficient effort. Finding an internship is hard work, but it's worthwhile and rewarding work. Following my process will lead to success in landing that internship.

Available Resources:

- http://www.huffingtonpost.com/claudia-chan/career-advice_b_2727157.html?utm_hp_ref=tw

- http://www.usnews.com/education/blogs/professors-guide/2010/03/31/10-tips-for-college-students-looking-for-a-job-in-a-tough-market

- http://www.jobdiagnosis.com/myblog/job-search-tips-for-college-students.htm

- http://jobs.aol.com/articles/2012/02/17/the-find-a-job-plan-for-college-seniors/

INTERN IMPACT ZONE 1

The Changing Landscape Of The Intern Experience

Marvism

Your life is a series of opportunities from which you will experience and learn from both your successes and failures.

The lessons of experience mold and shape our character. These lessons include successes and failures – pain and agony – fear and building confidence. Success in life will allow you to go forward with a willingness to own and manage each and every opportunity.

At this early juncture in your career, your learning platform will be enhanced with each internship you engage. However, you must understand what an intern is before you can experience it and learn from it to the maximum. *An internship is your opportunity to maximize the choices you have made in high school and/or college.* Your education is a catalogue of experiences that most likely included trial and error and success and failure. In this book I outline for you a method to assimilate these experiences in a formalized professional opportunity in which you should learn from others and learn from you own efforts. No matter the situation your internship and the experiences derived from it are yours to own and to manage. Further, you must manage how you respond to the ramifications of both the good and bad choices and decisions you have made in professional and educational life. And finally, your success is dependent on how you respond to the actions and choices others have made that directly impact your life.

By definition:

An internship is a supervised period and framework of professional work that provides both technical and practical personal and professional experience. We have evolved the definition in the last few years to say the internship is any opportunity that provides the following:

- Technical expertise in your chosen field of study

- General experience working in a more formal, foreign work environment than previously experienced

- Learning specific new skills that supplement a previous skill set

- Opportunity to practice new skills in a safe environment where both success and failure are expected as opportunities to learn

- Opportunity to demonstrate potential

- Experiencing a basic office structure including: arriving at work on time, appropriate office attire, getting along with coworkers

Internships are no longer limited or defined by the location of the intern verses the company. In our global, wired economy, remote or virtual internships are becoming more commonplace, up 20% from 2011 to 2012. In a virtual internship assignment, supervisions and team projects are managed online: similar to online or distance learning. Reduced commuting costs, flexible work hours, and the ability to take classes or work part-time are significant benefits of virtual internships.

The benefits of virtual internships must be balanced against the drawbacks.

There are many drawbacks to virtual internships, including minimal opportunity to develop office interpersonal skills, support and training to develop new skills, and verification of the validity of the virtual internship. You and your academic advisor must carefully analyze whether a remote internship meets your academic needs, as well as the university's requirements.

My philosophy is that whether the internship is paid or not paid, if you receive academic credit or if you simply receive work experience, each internship you complete will be successful when and only if the following conditions are met:

- The opportunity is structured – roles and responsibilities and performance measures are clearly stated and evaluated

- The opportunity has a prescribed duration

- You have defined specific personal and professional goals for yourself

- You and the organization have defined specific performance expectations that meet the SMARTS doctrine for objectives:

  - Specific

  - Measurable

  - Achievable

- Results-Oriented

- Time-Bound

- Stretch Your Capabilities

This book has been designed for students seeking internships who find themselves struggling to find opportunities with the deluge of competition seeking the same opportunities. Universities have many resources to assist students in these endeavors. They do an outstanding job of preparing students for the internship and career initiation skills needed for success. However, it must be understood that the university does not have an infinite source of companies willing to provide this learning experience. The best schools will always have the largest companies, often managed by alumni, with sophisticated internship programs. These programs will always gain the attention of students for a number of reasons – company name recognition, friend and fellow student's previous internship experience, the allure of potential job opportunities with big well-known companies.

Nevertheless, students and parents must understand that the search process does not begin and end with the university and it does not begin and end with the biggest, well-known organizations. The great majority of internship opportunities are going to come from much smaller organizations who do not have organized programs, that must be convinced that creating internship opportunities is an excellent business opportunity that can also provide a source of internal, organizational growth. The industries and functional areas available to you are immense and in many cases will not be on your university lists. Your success is driven by your willingness to own and manage your internship search and learn from the actual experience and leverage of the skills attained through the internship experience. My experience has proven that people like you, who understand what you can do and want to do to grow your professional career, create many of the best opportunities. This chart offers examples of industries and their functional disciplines and related internship opportunities, but by no means is exhaustive.

Industry Sample Internship Opportunities

Not-For-Profit Social Service Delivery Agencies - Examples: YMCA, Social Service Agencies

- Brand Management

- Membership Marketing

- Finance or Accounting

- Fund Raising Projects

- Social Media Development

- Annual Budget Development Projects

- Literacy Teaching/Tutoring

- Volunteerism

- Information Management

Not-For-Profit Association - Examples: Literacy League, Alumni Associations

- Brand Management and Rebranding

- Membership Marketing

- Finance or Accounting

- Fund Raising Projects

- Social Media Strategy

- Literacy Teaching/Tutoring

- Volunteerism

- Information Management

Not-for-Profit Healthcare - Example: Hospitals

- Administrative and Clinical Fellowships

- Clinical Internships

- Human Resources Internship
- Finance or Accounting
- Social Media Strategy
- Literacy Teaching/Tutoring
- Volunteerism
- Information Management

Real Estate Agencies

- Sales and Marketing
- Information Management
- Social Sales and Marketing

Small Local Retail

- Sales and Marketing
- Information Management
- Customer Relations
- Social Sales and Marketing
- Content Marketing

Radio, Television, Print Media

- Sales and Marketing
- Social Media Development
- Advertising
- Journalism
- Media Relations and Communications

Legal Firms

- Law Clerks
- Research Clerks
- Client Relations

Nursing Homes

- Administrative and Clinical Fellowships
- Clinical Internships
- Human Resources Internship
- Finance or Accounting
- Social Media Development
- Literacy Teaching/Tutoring
- Volunteerism
- Information Management

Manufacturing

- All Engineering Disciplines
- Communications
- Human Resources
- Finance or Accounting
- Social Media Development
- Literacy Teaching/Tutoring
- Information Management

Hospitality and Travel

- Marketing and Brand Management
- Event Planning and Management

- Human Resources

- Travel

- Finance or Accounting

- Social Sales and Marketing

Service

- Marketing and Brand Management

- Human Resources

- Finance and Accounting

- Social Media Development

- Information Management

Government

- Political Science

- Human Resources

- Finance or Accounting

- Social Media Development

- Information Management

- All Engineering Disciplines and Specialties

Sports

- Sports Management

- Sales and Marketing

- Media Relations

- Finance or Accounting

- Social Media Relations

- Information Management

Schools – Examples: Elementary, High Schools and Universities

- Sports Management

- Media Relations

- Finance or Accounting

- Social Media Development

- Information Management

- Marketing and Brand Management

- Event Planning and Management

- Human Resources

- Literacy Teaching/Tutoring

- Volunteerism

From the desk of the SVP Human Resources:

- An internship is your opportunity to maximize the choices you have made in high school and/or college. Seek to maximize your opportunity

- Employers believe that whether an internship is paid or not paid, if you receive academic credit or if you simply receive work experience, each internship you complete will be successful when and only if the following conditions are met:

    - The internship is structured – roles and responsibilities and performance measures are clearly stated and evaluated

    - The opportunity has a prescribed duration

    - You have defined specific personal and professional goals

    - You and the organization have defined specific performance expectations that meet the SMARTS doctrine for objectives: Specific, Measurable, Achievable, Time-bound and Stretches Your Capabilities

INTERN IMPACT ZONE 2

Internship Myth Busters

Marvism

We grow and learn by overcoming our Scotomas – our blind-spots where we place limits on our capabilities out of laziness, fear, habits, attitudes and false beliefs.

1.   MYTH BUSTER: All The Internships Are Gone

FACT: If it's late spring, summer is near and school is getting out soon and you don't have an internship or summer job, you're way behind and it is going to be tough to find one now. The opportunities available today are gone tomorrow. You must constantly be working the system. Most companies will hire interns if they are given a good reason and you are the right person. Internships are available every month of the year, if you know where to look and how to present yourself. And if they're hiring someone, why can't they hire you? If they aren't hiring, there still can be an internship for you. What I do not accept is the statement "all the internships are gone".

2.   MYTH BUSTER: You Need Connections To Get An Internship

FACT: You have more connections than you realize. Build your contact list and find connections within the businesses to get an internship. Internships don't always go to the best-qualified student, they go to the person who gets hired for the internship – there may be no logic! If you're looking for your first job after graduation, it's a competitive job market, and an internship allows you to gain valuable work experience, meet potential employers and learn on-the-job information about your chosen field.

3.   MYTH BUSTER: Our Field Does Not Have Internships And Others Make You Pay To Intern

FACT: Regardless of their size or field, companies want and need interns, they just might not know it yet. What they don't want are headaches and interns who don't take initiative, or aren't willing to work. Interning is a competitive market. Some students are paying for an internship, especially in technical areas! Adults undergoing career changes are competing with college students for internships to get their foot in the door.

4.   MYTH BUSTER: All Internships Are Unpaid

FACT: Some internships are paid, some are unpaid. Just as some are for school credit, and others are to gain valuable job experience. Your resume and a potential employer will appreciate valuable job experience whether you were paid or not paid. In fact, I believe when positioned properly, high quality work for no remuneration will be seen by many as a strong commitment to your professional development.

Of course, paid internships are the preference of all students but unfortunately we will find that the paid opportunities are few and most likely with larger companies or companies that are more financially profitable. Paid internships exist primarily in the private sector or in large organizations that have the money to pay students to learn while they work. Why do some organizations pay while others do not? The answer is simply because they can afford it, allowing them to differentiate the company and be competitive in attracting the best of the best candidates. There are various methods of remuneration including an hourly wage, salary or a stipend.

As discussed throughout the book, **laws prohibit companies hiring unpaid interns to replace paid workers.** There has recently been significant attention paid to these laws, even though they are not new laws. probably due to recent high unemployment. This has resulted in many companies re-thinking their internship policies and programs. In some cases, companies have eliminated internships while they re-evaluate their internship programs. In other companies, they have chosen to make all interns paid internships to ensure compliance.

You need to be aware of the issues concerning paid and unpaid internships and prepared to discuss your needs when the topic arises.

5.   MYTH BUSTER: An Internship Is Not A Real Job; You Just Make Coffee And Run Errands

FACT: An internship is a real job, and yes, sometimes interns are sent to Starbucks. And yes, there are some bosses that make coffee runs.

> *An internship is a valuable lesson into how companies really operate, and how to successfully interact with your co-workers and earn respect.*

Companies want interns who are eager to learn and who take initiative and don't just sit around and wait for something to do. Procrastination and laziness are the greatest reasons for failure. Think of your next internship as an extended job interview, and prove that bullet point on your resume that says you're "self-motivated."

The search for ways to be productive is invaluable in proving yourself. Don't expect to always be given a task; think of something productive to do while waiting for the next assignment.

If you are interning, develop a solid relationship with your boss and ask for regular meetings to get feedback and to learn from his or her experience. This is a solid step toward converting your experience to a full-time permanent opportunity when you graduate.

Engaging the boss and others will keep you in the forefront of their thoughts when an entry-level position becomes available.

Bottom-line: An internship should be undertaken as a long-term, sophisticated job interview.

Remember, this is a job and you're being evaluated. How you dress, perform and interact with your peers and superiors is always under scrutiny.

6. MYTH BUSTER: My Resume Should Only Be One Page Long

FACT: *Your resume should be the length it takes to tell your story* in clear, succinct and professional format. I hate this issue and I argue with students constantly. Career Centers seem to consistently tell students that your resume can only be one page. Those of us in business working for corporations disagree. You need to understand that your resume is vitally important and it is your documented history, and now your conduit into the mind of a potential hiring manager. You should also realize that interns are most often being evaluated for hiring by low-level recruiters from the HR department. A resume must be organized to demonstrate clearly the candidate's knowledge, skills, capabilities and successes. However, it must also be easily read, structured in a professional manner, using proper fonts and the right amount of space to tell your story, no more or less. If someone tells you they ignore resumes longer than one page, this means they aren't interested in finding the best candidates but are interested in arbitrary and capricious HR rules. Your resume should capture attention by what you say at first glance. I will spend a lot more time on resumes later.

7. MYTH BUSTER: The Only Internships Are At The Big, More Modern Companies.

FACT: Some of the best internships will be at small companies where you will have an opportunity to work with the most senior levels of the company and will probably be given more challenging assignments. Yes, the big name retail and box stores have that sexy allure and bragging rights. However, if you have self confidence and want unique experience that provides you the highest learning opportunity, the smaller company will probably provide you a much more meaningful experience. For example, if you want to be a marketing professional you could decide to seek an internship with a major clothing retailer that is in every mall in America. In this job, you will be one of dozens of interns doing very basic work as a part of a team of interns. On the other hand, you could be an assistant to the storeowner of a high-end retail boutique where you will learn entrepreneurial skills in addition to marketing skills within your field of study. My book will assist you with finding or creating these types of internship opportunities.

8. **MYTH BUSTER: You Can't Get An Internship As A High School Student.**

FACTS: There are no rules to the internship world. However, there are certain realities. Companies will always target upper-level college students for internships but under certain circumstance, there is room in the internship world even for the high school student. In fact, there are companies who design high school based internships to encourage career direction, especially in fields such as nursing, engineering and other sciences where there is scarcity of critical resources. Seeking an internship as a high school student is a challenge, but when successful, quite rewarding, as universities will admire your effort and maturity and it will strengthen your college application.

9. **MYTH BUSTER: You Should Only Take An Internship In The Field You Want To Pursue.**

FACTS: Insisting that you only want to do work in your field of choice is not very smart. Interning at a hospital if you plan on being a healthcare administrator is a great way to get your foot in the door. However, if you are having trouble tapping into a hospital as your preferred option, perhaps a nursing home or physical therapy center will also help acquire similar skills. If none of these are available, an opportunity outside of the industry might assist you in developing leadership skills transferable to any industry. Lets face it: We have all had jobs we don't necessarily like but we understand it's a job we need.

10. **MYTH BUSTER: Most Students Get Their Jobs and Internships Through On-Campus Recruiting.**

FACTS: Wrong. On-campus is the first place where most students look for an internship. This makes sense and it should be your first step but not your only source of opportunities. Corporations that come to campus to interview students provide an excellent resource for those seeking internship with companies with well-defined, sophisticated intern and hiring programs. However, universities agree that students secure at least 50% of their employment through means other than on-campus recruiting.

***

For most students, their unique interests and goals lead them in directions that require individualized approaches. This is why it is so important for students to meet with counselors and to understand the strategies needed to pursue their chosen path, and to develop their own customized job or internship search plans and proposals.

These myths challenge students each day in their pursuit of career success. By reading this book you will open yourself to greater opportunities and success.

From the desk of the SVP Human Resources:

- Many of the myths around internship come from real concerns, but these myths cannot be barriers to achieving success

- Employers always want you to be challenged on the job – they don't want you to be bored and they don't want to waste money

- Challenging internship myths is the best way to create your ideal internship – because it's probably not the what other students are doing – unless they've read this book

Define The Job You Want

Marvisim

The Most Successful and Meaningful Internship You Will Find Is The One You Create from your passion, your knowledge, skills and abilities and your drive to Find Your Intern Impact Zone!

The most successful and meaningful internship is the one that you define for yourself based upon your knowledge, skills, abilities and interests.

Define Your Ideal Internship. To be successful you must be prepared to be flexible in the type of internship you are willing to accept. If making money is an imperative, your entire strategy may be different than if you desire work experience or to meet academic requirements. Also, consider that some schools such as Notre Dame or BYU require service projects as part of your academic work. If this is part of your need then you should try to find an opportunity that permits both service and experience in your field of endeavor. You must consider the goals you have set for this experience:

Goal I: To gain valuable, general work experience, or

Goal II: To gain specific experience in a given field of study or needed expertise, or

Goal III: To complete a service project, or

Goal IV: Elements of Goal I or II and to make money - the most difficult scenario

Example of Creating Your Own Internship:

Jane is a business major, with a concentration in Human Resources. She has typical student work experience as a waitress and as a baby-sitter. At the time of her internship search, she had no professional experience in her field of study. Jane's ideal internship was to work in an environment where she would gain experience as a HR professional. While she desired a paid opportunity, she realized it was more important to gain experience. She also realized that attaining a job in a professional HR environment would be difficult. She is also required to do a service project in support of the underprivileged. Jane decided to focus on the following strategies:

- Interview on campus for as many opportunities as possible, providing valuable interviewing experience and she might land one of these positions

- Search for small manufacturing companies in her geographic area where she can assist doing basic Human Resources work such as assisting in recruitment of entry level positions or do a project in areas such as benefits and recruitment

- Search for a series of not-for-profits with small, 2 or 3 person HR departments who could benefit from projects such as creating or updating employee manuals or documentation of HR processes

- Include in the search not-for-profits whose focus is to provide service to those in need; therefore, the agencies in her area might include: YMCA's, Center for Women in Distress or other United Way Agencies

From the desk of the SVP Human Resources:

- To be successful you must be prepared to be flexible in the type of internship you are willing to accept

- If making money is an imperative, your entire strategy may be different than if you desire work experience or to meet academic requirements

- Not all businesses will be able to provide you the ideal opportunity you desire, but that doesn't mean there is not great value in being flexible

INTERN IMPACT ZONE 4

Target Company Research

Target company research can be a time consuming effort. This research should be in addition to social media research and the development of your LinkedIn networking efforts. You have already discovered that your career development department within your academic institution has tremendous resources including lists of internship programs and opportunities posted by the largest companies. While these are highly competitive opportunities, they should not be ignored or confused with the efforts defined in this book.

However, you must realize that these opportunities represent a small portion of the potential opportunities available to you through my process. Remember, the majority of businesses and companies do not have formal internship programs. This does not mean that these companies do not want internship programs. There are many reasons why they are not sponsoring formal internships. Some of the best opportunities might lie in the smallest business environments. Do not allow yourself to be swayed by the size and name of the company. The following steps should assist you in identifying companies to approach with your proposal:

1. Identity your preferred geographic location for your internship

2. Identify local sources for lists of small companies in your target area. The following sources have lists of companies or company CEO's:

    - Chambers of Commerce

    - Junior Leagues

    - Rotary Clubs

    - Not-for-Profits

    - Local Business Journal

    - Local Crain's Business

    - LinkedIn Company Research by Zip Code and Company Size

3. Identify the highest level of individuals within these companies that you have chosen

4. Research the demographics of these targeted businesses and how they might fit within your ideal internship

Example:

- My target geographic area: Greater Boca Raton Area in Florida

- My target internship: A social service delivery internship

- My target sources:

    - Boca Raton Chamber of Commerce

    - Delray Beach Chamber of Commerce

    - Boynton Beach Chamber of Commerce

    - United Way Agency

    - Palm Beach Post Gazette

    - LinkedIn Zip Code Search

- Internet research to find not-for-profit companies listed with each of these associations

- Internet research on the not-for-profit companies - find names of executive and department directors

- Target not-for-profits meeting your internship requirements

WARNING: Watch out for Suspicious Internship Opportunities

You should be careful to assess the legitimacy of each internship opportunity - particularly virtual internships as discussed earlier. There are some employers who use the word *internship* as a disguise for what are actually part-time jobs for which anyone can apply. Your internship should NOT be anything simple busy work that no one else in the office wants to do. Also, there are many employers who use the term *internship* to describe what is actually nothing more than a high-turnover sales position. Remember, an internship should be opportunity to learn on the job. The following are a few tips to consider to make sure your opportunity is the right opportunity:

- The company should be easily referenced on the Internet or listed with the Better Business Bureau

- The internship should not be focused on sales with a promise of high incentive earnings

- A reputable company should review your qualifications as much as you should check out the company

- A legitimate internship will be posted in reputable places; internships posted on flyers and passed around campus are likely not to be of the quality you want or need

- Use social media sites, The Better Business Bureau, Chambers of Commerce, Google Maps and other government and civic entities to verify addresses of small companies and those doing business from a residence, especially when going for an interview

From the desk of the SVP Human Resources:

- Use every opportunity to secure the best internship for you and to learn and improve your job search skills

- Some of the best internships will come from small business environments and not-for-profit environments

- Be prudent in your research, making sure that the company and opportunity provide a valid environment for you to work

The Art, Science And Importance Of A Resume

Marvism

Your resume provides a well-defined roadmap of your professional and personal path of experience, capability and development. This roadmap should be specific and include the details required to understand your qualifications with the brevity required to demonstrate your writing skills and ability to convey relevant information.

The Myth: Hiring managers and Human Resources professionals will not accept a resume over one page.

Myth Buster: As I said previously, your resume should be the length necessary to describe to the reader what you've done, what you want to do and what you can do in a concise, professional format. A resume is a summary of your qualifications that supports and defines your qualifications for the position for which you are applying. It serves as your primary marketing tool, defining what you have to offer and along with a supporting cover letter, creates the foundation of a potential employer's first impression of you.

Your resume should be concise, yet provide sufficient information to entice the potential employer to pursue your candidacy. Each word, every phrase, defines you and is validation that you are not only qualified but also possibly the best candidate for the internship or job you desire.

Your resume is a snapshot that lives indefinitely in the minds of employers! It creates an image of you as a person and your capabilities. So you must ask yourself: *What is the image you want others to have of you.* Consider these points:

- A person who presents himself or herself with clarity

- A person who pays attention to details

- A person who possesses strong grammatical and spelling skills

- A person who has specific technical, interpersonal and professional skills

- A person who makes an affirmative personal statement regarding his or her knowledge, skills, abilities and talents

I'm disappointed and amazed at a great number of hiring managers, Human Resources recruiters and career development professionals who lack the intellectual veracity and practical professional knowledge to appreciate that the objective of a resume is to accurately convey the experience, qualifications and capabilities of an individual in a clear and concise manner in consideration for a job or internship, regardless of length. When I have heard these individuals declare without forethought or valid experience that a resume in no case should be longer than one page I am appalled. In my opinion, to so narrowly apply such an arbitrary standard, is to say that they are not interested in knowing your skills and your successes that may lend themselves to your success on the job.

"I made this letter longer than usual because I lack the time to make it short."

~Mark Twain —> Blaise Pascal

I've interviewed and hired thousands of people over the last 30-years and recruiters under my direction have hired tens of thousands more. In no case would I permit the dismissal of a candidate merely because their resume exceeded one page. So lets get real; if this is the standard of a corporation and the attitude of a hiring manager or HR professional and you want the job, you will need to comply. But I still question the logic.

Resume Planning and Composition

In a great number of cases it may be necessary to have two or even three versions of a resume. This is necessary when your search for a position may be in differing industries and types of companies. Your resume is your story – the question, of course, is how you are going to tell your story. However, in telling your story you must be sure that by the end of your resume the following questions have been answered to the hiring manager's satisfaction:

- Your professional objective, including the correlation of this objective with the internship you are seeking

- An accurate account of the specific skills that you possess, delineating clearly what you are bringing to the company to which you are applying, including classes and trainings you have completed

- An accurate account of your work history including dates and descriptions of responsibilities and successes, as appropriate, including volunteer positions and previous internships

- An accurate account of your affiliations, memberships, awards and recognitions

Resume development requires a career focused strategy followed by a sound writing construction process. The strategy process begins with taking a personal inventory of all the foundational elements and skill potential within your life. With an analysis of your experience, knowledge, skills, accomplishments and interests, your resume will be a professional statement that will impress anyone who reads it.

The following is a list of sections that your resume should contain:

1. **Contact Information:** Your contact information is a very important component that introduces you to a prospective employer. Your contact information should contain the following:

    - Your name in a larger type than the rest of your resume

    - Your home city and state – do not include your street address for security purposes

    - Your phone number where you can be contacted. Note: Make sure your voice mail greeting contains a professional message to callers. Tip: Google Voice has free telephone numbers that you could use to differentiate personal from business calls.

    - Your email address

2. **Professional Objective:** This is a clear, concise statement of your specific internship aspiration. It can be seen as your Call To Action. It tells the employer what you want – the job you desire.

    Your professional objective is not a statement
    about your future career –
    It is about "now," not later.

    Your statement should be in sync with your cover letter. I strongly suggest that when possible make your statement specific to each internship you are proposing or to each job you are applying.

3. **Education:** Recruiting professionals suggest that your educational history should be placed at the beginning of your resume if your educational qualifications are significant or from a renowned university. Include in this section the names of schools, dates attended, degrees and dates received, and major and minor fields of study and grades.

27

Internships, fellowships and practicums are also ideal for this section. You should also include in this section relevant course work to give the employer a clearer sense of your job-related skills.

4. **Professional Experience:** Include in the experience section names of employers, dates of work including month and year, job titles and functional areas where you've worked and your accomplishments. Listing accomplishments is very important. Accomplishments should be quantifiable or a statement that demonstrates how you made a difference in the work environment. This can also include a key or significant learning accomplishment achieved. Include part-time jobs held during your high school and college years. This category can include volunteerism, internships, fellowships or practicum experiences, if not contained within the education section. Use strong wording that describes your work experience in results-oriented terms:

- Restaurant Server: Customer-focused wait-staff service provider

- Head-Start Daycare Volunteer: Responsible and sensitive daycare volunteer

- Healthcare Administrative Fellow: Detail-oriented and business-focused intern

5. **Professional and Social Affiliations and Awards:** This section details your social and professional activities that demonstrate achievements and any awards that you have attained outside of the academic or professional experience sections. You should also include professional memberships, awards, honors, hobbies, volunteer experience and community service. Use this section when you have sufficient activity and recognition to be contained in a separate heading.

6. **Professional and Technical Skills:** The content of this section can be used in various ways. Professional and technical skills are relevant in an attempt to define very specific skills that you want an employer to know you have. A list of skills you could use is listed in the Resume Preparation Exercise at the end of this chapter.

7. **Other Relevant Experience:** This is an optional section that can include languages, sports, travel and other relevant extracurricular activities.

8. **References:** There are multiple opinions as to how references should be handled. In general, it is suggested that the statement, "References

Available Upon Request" be used in most resumes. However, if your references are particularly noteworthy they can be listed. In any case, insure that you asked and notified references of your need for their support in advance of including them on your resume. Make sure you tell your references the nature of the internship and attributes to mention that may be helpful when they are contacted.

Do's and Don'ts of Resume Writing

Do's

- Avoid using a wizard or template to create your resume – you don't want your resume identical to every other resume

- Each section of your resume should start with the most recent education, experience or activity to the oldest

- If you are printing your resume, use high-quality white or off-white paper

- Use a standard font (example Arial) for your resume – avoid fancy serf fonts

- Text size or your font should be 10–12-points, your name and headings can be larger, 12 points, and the body 10 points

- Be cautious about overuse of italics and boldface, and be consistent—if you use boldface type for one job title, do so for all job titles

- Explain any acronyms you use in your resume the first time you mention them, unless the term is a generally known standard or a standard within a given industry that you are applying

- Include only information relating to your education, skills, professional interests, and work experience, using short sentences and paragraphs - no more than 3 or 4 lines per paragraph

- Use indented statements with bullets, as a general guideline each bullet point should be at least five words and no more than three lines long

- Use quantities, numbers and dollar values when possible to demonstrate successes or scope of responsibilities

- Use action words such as *contributed, managed, developed, led, operated* to describe your responsibilities

- Put the strongest statements or qualifications at the top

- Have someone with strong English spelling and grammar skills check your spelling, grammar and punctuation

- Always…be creative and original without being gimmicky or offensive. For example, if you're applying for an internship in social sales and marketing, a QR code with your contact info is not gimmicky: It demonstrates your understanding of current social sales strategies.

Don'ts

- Don't try to impress with big, fancy words or jargon

- Don't use gimmicks. But stay aware of evolving resume trends such as the Twesume or @TweetMyResume that you might be required to use as part of your internship application

- Don't use photos of yourself unless requested

- Don't include salary history unless requested

- Don't include personal information such as: religion, national origin, or political affiliations

- Don't use pronoun "I" repeatedly to describe your responsibilities

A Twesume is your resume in 140 characters - or less - and is becoming popular with companies who use social recruiting.

In the appendix of this book you will find models of resumes that have proven successful and those that DO NOT meet the standard for success.

Santa Claus: World traveler and toy expert. 300+ years management experience. Looking for position in entertainment industry. http://tinyurl.com/c9ursdp #twesume

*~ **Mashable***

Resume Preparation Exercise

Before you start writing a resume or revising your old resume, you must ask yourself and document the answers to several important questions. The answers to these questions will assist you with both building your resume and with your interview skills preparation that we will discuss later. Your resume is telling your story in words. Do not think of it as a list of stuff you did, but instead think of it as an outline of your personal and professional development and the skills you have attained. A resume by its nature gives you "bragging rights" about your successes. You want this story to be a compelling testament that will be delivered in non-narrative, outline format.

1. **What are your interpersonal, professional and technical strengths – those things that a hiring manager will be impressed with – those things your professors, coaches and parents tell you that you're exceptionally good at doing?**

Examples:

- Organizational skills

- Verbal and written communications

- Leadership and managerial skills

- Teamwork

- Math and statistical acumen

- Planning

- Research and analytical skills

- Creativity and problem solving skills

2. *List your interpersonal, professional and technical strengths:*

_____

_____

_____

3. *What courses or training programs have you completed that contribute to your capabilities?*

_____

_____

_____

4. *What are the reasons a hiring manager will want to hire you for this internship or for a job?* The answer to this question is NOT, because "I work hard and I'm smart." The answer to this question must have substance. The answer goes to the core of who you are and what knowledge, skills and abilities you will bring to the job. This answer should be revealed within your resume and will be revealed within your interviews. The following are several examples of answers to this question:

   • Someone will want to hire me because I am an independent, responsible thinker who makes good personal decisions in life as demonstrated by being elected student body president and volunteering as a peer mentor

   • Someone will want to hire me because I have expert Word, Excel, Power-Point and presentation skills and have practice putting those skills to use in a marketing campaign

   • Someone will want to hire me because I have been a student-athlete who has demonstrated the ability to manage the demands of sports competition combined with being academically successful

   • Someone will want to hire me because I am academically accomplished, well organized and serve as a leader amongst my peers

   • Someone will want to hire me because I completed a 6-month social media internship in a digital marketing agency

   • In addition to my business management course work, I have worked at a fast-food restaurant and women's clothing retail store and gained valuable experience providing customer service and learning sales skills

An employer will want to hire me because:

_____

_____

_____

5. *In each job that you have had, list in one sentence the greatest accomplishment/success or greatest skill learned or greatest challenge that came from this job.* This answer should be directly stated within your resume and will be indirectly revealed within your interviews. The following are several examples of answers to this question:

- Consistently performed academically in the top 10% of my class in both high school and college

- A successful student-athlete in both high school and college, maintaining both academic and athletic standards expected with the institution including lettering in 2 sports while making the honor roll 6 semesters of high school

List several of your greatest accomplishments or greatest skills or challenges:

_____

_____

_____

6. **Using not more than three sentences define your greatest disappointment, challenge, mistake or improvement opportunity.** The following are several examples of answers to this question:

- As a senior in high school, it was my great desire to attend the University of Notre Dame on a football scholarship. When I at first did not get in, I had to regroup and make the decision to go to a college preparatory school to improve my grades and college entrance examination scores and reapply to ND. My plan was successful and I learned a lot about hard work and myself and attended Notre Dame on athletic scholarship.

- During my freshman year in college, my father died. In order to stay in school I needed to get a job and begin searching for other tuition sources. Now I am a senior honors student and still working my way through school and I've been able to secure several scholarships to assist in my tuition. Today, I'm a mature adult and ready to be a leader in any environment in which I work.

7. *List several of your greatest accomplishments or greatest skills or challenges:*

_____

_____

_____

The answers to each of these questions provide insight into your skills and perseverance in the face of adversity or challenges. Interviewers are not just looking for a list of jobs you've performed. They want to know your successes and the qualities you possess to overcome the odds that might make the average person give up and take the easy way out.

Your resume should use words that convey actions that d emonstrate your accomplishments and how your achievements and successes define you as a professional and your willingness and desire to translate your experiences into skills a potential employer will want to use.

From the desk of the SVP Human Resources:

Employers read thousands of resumes, therefore your resume must bring attention to you and tell your story in the most concise but thorough way possible, without using gimmicks

Resume writing is an art form that takes time to perfect, remember that "one size does not fit all" therefore be prepared to have resumes that meet various situations and business opportunities

Available Online Resources:

- http://hr.conquent.com/blog/index.cqs?blogid=1aee6e70d19711dfa529865b4ae2cd4e

- http://jobsearch.about.com/od/resumes/resumes.html

INTERN IMPACT ZONE 6

Create An Internship Proposal

After defining your ideal internship, you must create an **Internship Proposal**. Your proposal is the package you will submit for consideration to prospective internship employers. The quality of your proposal is the basis of your search. Each element plays a specific role in achieving your internship goals.

Your internship proposal has several objectives:

- Defines your internship and career goals

- Specifies the knowledge, skills, abilities and talents that you currently possess

- Identifies the new knowledge, skills, abilities and talents that you hope to attain

- Details duties and responsibilities that you propose to accomplish in the internship

- Defines how your success will be measured

- Assures the company that their investment in time and effort will be beneficial to the company

Internship Proposal Tools and Documents

The following is a list and description of the specific Internship Proposal tools and documents you need to develop to submit to the company. The development of these tools and documents will be beneficial now and in the future as your career develops and expands:

1. **Create A One-Page Job Description.** This job description has two primary objectives:

   a. Defines what your ideal internship looks like and defines the benefits that both you and your employer will derive from the experience. This description will save your prospective employer time figuring out what you want and can do. Of course, the employer will have the opportunity to adjust the focus of the job.

b.   Elements of Your Internship Job Description

    i.   **Internship Title:** This title should contain the word *Internship*

    ii.   **Internship Duration:** This is the proposed length and timeframe of the internship

    iii.   **Proposed Reporting Relationship**: Proposes the title or type of position to which this internship will report

    iv.   **Company**: This section identifies the name of the company and includes a brief paragraph describing the company

    v.   **Internship Job Summary**: This section is a one-paragraph summary of the position that you desire and must be flexible to allow the company to adjust or compromise to meet their business needs as well as your needs

    vi.   **Specific Intern Duties**: This is a list of specific duties and assignments and describes the details and way in which duties will be carried out

    vii.   **Education Requirements**: This is a list of the education requirements needed to fulfill the duties listed

    viii.   **Specific Technical Skills Required**: This is a list of specific skills required including items such as computer and software skills, writing skills, verbal presentation skills, etc

    ix.   **Proposed Remuneration**: This section should be well thought out and demonstrate flexibility, describing remuneration requested in the form of a lump sum stipend, an hourly wage or project completion payment or academic credit

Samples of an Internship Job Descriptions are in the Appendix. You can use these examples to assist in creating your job descriptions.

Warning: U.S. labor laws prohibit an unpaid intern from replacing what would otherwise be a paid position within the company. The ideal intern position is one that focuses on a project that would otherwise not be completed if your internship did not exist. Project work with a beginning and ending point and clear measures of success are ideal and meet the legal standard.

2. **Create A One-Page Performance Evaluation Form.** Your college or university may have a required form for this section that you are obligated to use, if you are doing an internship for credit. The problem with these required forms is that they do not necessarily fit within the structure of the company or may be too laborious or narrative driven. In these cases, I find this requirement to be a barrier to a company's acceptance of your proposal. I recommend that if the internship is designed to fit specific university requirements, propose to your academic advisor or responsible faculty member adjustments and options that meet the expectations of the employer. The following are the proposed elements of your evaluation form.

    a. Internship Title

    b. Intern Name

    c. Evaluation Period

    d. Internship Objectives

    e. Specific Deliverables and Performance Rating Criteria

    f. Specific Behavior and Skill Demonstration and Performance Rating Criteria

    g. General Narrative Impressions

    h. Reporting and Supervising Roles and Positions

    i. A sample of an Internship Job Evaluation is contained in the Appendix.

3. **Create a One-Page Letter of Introduction**: This letter will introduce you to the company and introduce your internship proposal. **Your letter of introduction is as important as your resume.** Remember, your prospective employer will probably see this letter before he or she sees your resume.

    The focus of this letter is to capture the employer's attention, to demonstrate your purpose, and to provide a good first impression. The letter draws the employer's attention to your interest, desire and commitment to the intern position. It should also highlight the most significant aspects of your background and experience that are relevant to the position and to the employer's needs. The letter should never be more than one page. The introduction enables you to:

    a. Direct/target your resume to a specific person

    b.   Provide additional information about yourself as it might relate to the specific position for which you are applying

    c.   Briefly describe your knowledge of the job and potential employer

    d.   Clearly Indicates what follow-up action(s) you will take

    e.   If you have been referred by a specific person for your internship and have their permission, the letter of introduction is the place where you should share this information

Do's and Don'ts of Writing Your Intern Letter of Introduction

- Use plain stationary and the same format as your resume

- Demonstrate warmth and sincerity

- Avoid jargon and overused phrases

- Do not hand-write your letter

The following are the elements of your Letter of Introduction

a. Date and contact information

b. Paragraph I: Introduce yourself and your objective

c. Paragraph II: Introduce your internship proposal - set up your Call to Action

d. Paragraph III: Explain the benefits of your proposal

e. Paragraph IV: Call to Action

f. Paragraph V: Conclusions – describe your plans for follow up and thank you

Samples of an Internship Letter of Introduction are contained within the Appendix.

From the desk of the SVP Human Resources:

- An internship proposal gives you a unique opportunity to create the ideal internship

- Employers will respect and appreciate your initiative and creativity when you take the time to understand and anticipate their needs and expectations

- Creating a proposal can be especially beneficial when presented to a small business environment where a defined internship program does not exit

Available Online Resources:

- http://www.mountainstate.edu/students-current/career-services/documents/02.09.11%20EXAMPLE%20PROPOSAL.pdf

- http://www.docstoc.com/docs/4229272/Internship-Proposal-Example-(1)

- http://www.ithaca.edu/business/docs/internship_docs/sample_intern_prop.pdf

- http://ryancdavidson.com/blog/2010/05/what-does-an-internship-proposal-look-like/

INTERN IMPACT ZONE 7

Assembling Your Proposal

Your Internship Proposal must be presented in a professional manner, serving as a demonstration of the detail and quality of your work. The following details are imperative for success:

1. Spelling and Grammar

    a. Spelling and grammar must be checked, rechecked and preferably reviewed by someone else

    b. Each document should have the same font, color, size and margins

2. Structure

    a. Each document should have a professional header including the name of the document, internship title, intern's name and date created

    b. Each document over one page should have a professional footer including your name and page number on additional pages

3. Presentation

    a. Proposal should be prepared for presentation in both an electronic and hardcopy format

        a. Hardcopy Format

            i.   Print each document separately

            ii. Assemble the package in a plastic binder with a clear cover and a dark back

            iii. Your introduction letter should not be in the binder

            iv. Remember, most universities offer a printing service to assist you

        b. Electronic Format

            i.   Your Letter of Introduction will be your email body

    ii.   Your resume, job description and evaluation will be attachments to your Letter of Introduction

        1.   Make sure each attachment to your letter is clearly referenced at the end of your letter with the statement, "Attached below is my resume, a proposed job description and proposed evaluation form."

        2.   Make sure attachments are in the same order as they have been referenced in your letter

        3.   Each document attached should be saved and attached as PDF to insure that the formatting remains intact

Sending Your Proposal to Targeted Companies

Your Target Company Research has assisted you in finding the environments that you feel meet your needs and expectations. Without a specific internship posting or a recommended contact person, interns often find it difficult to find to whom you should send your proposal and how to address each person. The answer to this question is situational. The following guidelines and recommendation will assist you.

Large Companies:

    a.   Normally the Human Resources Department

    b.   Refer to the company's online job posting system for guidance

Small Companies:

    a.   Directly contact the owner of the company

    b.   Manager of HR

    c.   Location or department managers

From the desk of the SVP HR

- Employers realize that maneuvering through a corporation to find an internship can be an intimidating and daunting task – nevertheless the task is yours to manage. Your persistence in finding the right channels demonstrates your initiative and purpose.

INTERN IMPACT ZONE 8

The Art, Science and Importance of the Follow-Up and Thank You

You must be prepared to follow-up on each proposal that you submit. Your timing will be very important. This follow-up is key to your proposal staying in the forefront of the potential employer's thoughts. Your follow-up letter should be brief and should verify that your proposal was received.

A follow-up thank you letter is also important after all interviews, expressing your appreciation for the interview and reconfirming your interest in the company.

The following guidelines will help you to develop follow-up and thank you letters:

- Send a follow-up letter to prospective employers to whom you have sent proposals approximately 10 days to 2 weeks after your proposal should have been received

- Send your thank you letter within 24-hours of your interview if possible

- Be personal, specific and genuine in your appreciation for the time of the interviewer

- Note specific points of the conversation you had with the interviewer to demonstrate you listened, appreciated the conversation and enjoyed learning about the company and the opportunity

- Correct any significant misunderstanding you may have realized after the interview

- Confirm follow-up actions and commitments such as: *As you requested, I will provide you a copy of my marketing project by Friday, June 21, 2013*

Sample Follow-Up and Thank You Letters are contained within the Appendix.

From the desk of the SVP Human Resources:

- Following up with persons you've interviewed with or have made a connection is a demonstration of professionalism and what can be expected of you when you are on the job

Available Online Resources:

- http://jobsearch.about.com/od/thankyouletters/a/thankinterview.htm

- http://www.career.vt.edu/Interviewing/AfterThanksFollowUp.html

The Art, Science And Importance
Of The 30-Second Elevator Speech

Marvism

A Strong 30-Second Elevator Speech Can Make the Difference in the Rest of Your Career.

There will be countless times during your career when you will need to introduce yourself to an individual or group of people. This is an important technique that you must master. It will be the difference in opening the door and impressing people verses being just another voice in the crowd. A 30-second introduction should become one of your skills, adaptable to multiple situations. Anytime someone says "Tell me about yourself", you must be prepared to provide a professional, yet at times a more personalized statement of who you are. We call this speech an "Elevator Pitch" because it describes the challenge you have if you had to introduce yourself from the moment you step into an elevator and the door closed until the time the elevator reached its destination and the doors open. A word to the wise – we aren't talking about an elevator ride to the top of Empire State Building. Generally speaking we only have 30-60 seconds to make a powerful first impression. The attention span of the average person is just 30 seconds before their mind starts wandering. Therefore, you must get the person's attention with a strong statement of who you are. Here is a series of helpful tips:

- **Get to the point, Be concise:** Your pitch should take no longer than 30-60 seconds

- **Be Clear:** Use language that everyone understands; fancy words don't make you look smarter

- **Demonstrate Strength:** Use words that are powerful and strong and grab attention

- **Tell Your Story:** Describe who you are, what you can do and how you get the job done

- **Call to Action:** Drive and encourage a specific action to engage you to the person to whom you are speaking

A top-notch, professional elevator speech is designed with a specific outcome in mind, captures the attention of the listener and Calls Them To Action – in others words makes them want to see you again

10 Steps to Develop Your Elevator Speech

1. Write out your elevator speech to insure the elements blend together in a shorter story. Write multiple versions of the speech. Try to be creative and don't hold back. The more ideas you have the better your final product will be.

_____

_____

_____

2. Write a short anecdote or story that demonstrates your strength and commitment. Don't worry if the story is too long, write it down for now.

_____

_____

_____

3. Write down your objective or goal. Example: my short-term goal is to secure an internship that will provide a step toward my career goal of working in the financial service sector.

_____

_____

_____

4. Develop a series of action statements. These statements should reflect your objectives or goals listed in #3.

_____

_____

_____

5.   Record yourself reading your draft statements. How do you sound? What really hits you? Which ones make you say, "I love that."

6.   Now relax for a while. Go work on some of the other tools in this book and come back to your drafts after your mind has cleared.

7.   Review your draft work. Begin to piece the good stuff together into a solid flow that makes sense and sounds conversational.

8.   Record your new drafts. By now, they will start sounding like you. Start paying attention to length. Remember, 30-seconds – not more than 60.

9.   Practice makes perfect. Dry run your final version of your elevator speech to family and friends. This is hard but it's worth the effort – feedback will be crucial in your professional world. If you can't give your elevator speech to family, how will you give it to total strangers, in unfamiliar surroundings?

10.   Memorize, practice and use the speech as often as possible.

Remember several final points. We do not speak the way we write. So your speech must be written as if you are saying it out loud in a conversation. This is not a simple task: Successful business people spend years perfecting and revising their elevator speeches. There are books and courses dedicated to elevator speeches, and some people hire professional career coaches and speechwriters to write theirs. But with practice, you should be able to write and perfect your own.

Case Study

Rachel is a 15-year-old martial arts Intern-Instructor. This teen may not be typical thanks to her parents and perhaps a little to the impact and influence of her supportive extended family of 20+ aunts and uncles and 25+ first cousins: I will give her godparents a little play as well since that refers to my wife and me. Completing her sophomore year in high school, this teenager may be far beyond typical in terms of her interpersonal development through a myriad of extracurricular activities. Her parents and extended family are well educated and you would have to define the family as academically, professionally and socially competitive.

Rachel's activities, beyond the demands of attending a highly competitive high school, include participating on both the high school and club level volleyball teams. But her engagement doesn't stop there. She is also an accomplished flutist, participating in the high school concert band all year and in the marching band in the volleyball off-season. She has sung in the children's choir at her local church, is now a communion server and is completing her 10th year of German language training she started at age 5.

Rachel's greatest and most impressive accomplishment is her physical talent and mental discipline demonstrated as 2nd degree black belt in Tae Kwon Do, a sport she began in 2nd grade. What her parents and instructor realize about the teen is her commitment and ability to follow direction and be responsible and accountable. Her dad is also an accomplished martial artist, "I started RW in the martial arts to support her growth and maturity as she grows into a woman. We wanted her to be disciplined in life and of course I wanted her to have the ability to protect herself in the worst case scenario." However, her father added, what became a natural outgrowth of the martial arts is the leadership capabilities and development.

Grand Master Kim, the owner of W. Kim Tae Kwon Do & Hapkido of Palatine, Illinois, said, "It's normal to hire students who have achieved certain levels to be instructors for lower level students. However, it is not normal to have an instructor at age 14." Grand Master Kim realizes the value added by a young instructor such as Rachel, but he also acknowledged that she has much to learn. RW's responsibilities are considered those of a paid intern. Under the direction and scrutiny of a senior instructor, she spends 3 to 5 hours per week leading classes, always under the watchful eye of her mentor. From the standpoint of the Grand Master and RW's parents, there are multiple benefits:

- Development of leadership skills

- Verbal, behavioral and social self-assurance

- Professional verbal skills that will be valuable in her academic endeavors and later in her career growth

- Balancing and expanding her resume and application for college

- Discipline and preparation for the rigors of academic life

Rachel feels her instructor's feedback has been a message that she has become very accomplished in the martial arts, but she also feels that it has a message of self-confidence, "At first I was nervous even though I knew what to do. After a few classes, I started to feel like a leader and I knew that I had to show that I had confidence. The kids younger than me were easy for me, but leading adults was different. I had to earn their respect. Master Kim and my dad helped me learn ways to give them instruction. I learned that all people are different and people learn in different ways."

The Grand Master Kim noted other important points regarding his philosophy, "We have rules and expectations of all students. These are posted on our walls. When you join our club, you must follow these rules. They apply here, at home, at school and at work. As an Intern-Instructor, I expect even more of RW and other instructors. She must set an example for my students and for her peers in her studies and behavior. My job is not just to teach Tae Kwon Do, my job is to teach leadership and responsibility. We use Tae Kwon Do as the teaching tool." Grand Master Kim and the W. Kim Tae Kwon Do and Hapkido School fulfill each of the requirements defined as core elements of an internship.

- Teaches new skills

- Provides a benefit to the intern over and above basic work requirements

- Works under close supervision of more experienced staff

- Provides training that derives no immediate advantage to the organization; and on occasion the development of the young student can actually impede what could otherwise be a more smoothly run organizational operation

- Realizes that the internship is not a guarantee of full-time permanent work at the conclusion of the internship

- Realizes that the intern is not entitled to wages for the time spent in the internship, but in this case the employer sees the value of monetary reward for performance

This paid internship will be an on-going opportunity for Rachel and assuming continuous improvement will allow her more hours and training in the summer. As a part of her development, Rachel is encouraged and coached how to verbally articulate the content and value of the experience. This discovery will prove invaluable and a differentiator as Rachel competes for college acceptance and career development.

More importantly, this case demonstrates that in the right circumstances internships can begin earlier in life and the development of leadership skills is something that is cultivated and used in multiple context environments and circumstances.

Rachel's next internship challenge is to secure an opportunity in a community service environment. This will be a requirement and leverage point in her applications for college. The following is Rachel's 30-second elevator speech:

> *"I'm a very active and I think successful high school sophomore. I'm an honors student and also a student-athlete. I'm on the volleyball team and I'm a flutist in both the marching and concert bands. Probably most fun and special to me is having been named an instructor at my Tae Kwon Do club.*

I've been active in Tae Kwon Do since the 2ⁿᵈ gr
having studied German for 10 years, I especially e
visit family. My longer-term goal is to attend col
Notre Dame and then go on to grad school where I
working in physical rehabilitation."

Begin your draft of your 30-Second Elevator Speech:

_____

_____

_____

From the desk of the SVP Human Resources:

- Employers watch for those who are able to present themselves professionally in a clear concise manner

- Your elevator speech demonstrates not only your ability to introduce yourself as a potential intern, it will also be a tool you will use throughout your career when dealing with clients and colleagues

Available Online Resources:

- http://www.youtube.com/watch?v=98WlZJqscVk

- http://office.microsoft.com/en-us/word-help/3-steps-to-a-great-elevator-pitch-HA010074786.aspx

Impact With Your Business Card

Another critical tool for your internship search is a business card. Many people think a business card is only for the person who has a job. But let's understand why people use these cards:

- Provides a professional image

- Provides another tool to market yourself

- Provides a reminder of who you are and possibly at the end of the day you end up in the address book of an executive or a hiring manager

- Provides an additional networking opportunity

- Communicates vital information about you

- Easy to carry with you

Business cards are small and inexpensive to buy or produce yourself and when correctly designed communicate vital information about you and your internship search. Even in our electronic age where our smart phones track our every step, the business card will differentiate you from others seeking an internship:

Side 1

- Name

- School, Major, Year

- Email

- Phone number

- LinkedIn address

Side 2

- Name

- Internship goal

To make your business card professional but distinctive - but not gimmicky - consider adding:

- QR code - an easy way to demonstrate you're tech and marketing savvy

- Personal photo: while I don't recommend your photo on your resume, it's perfectly acceptable on a business card provided the photo is professional and conveys your business persona

- Image of your original work: in creative fields a photo of fashion, art, film or other piece you've created that demonstrates your internship goals

Your business card should be professional and classic, unless you're in a highly creative field such as graphic design or art where your creativity is what you're offering. *Business cards are intended to be easily and quickly read, then saved for future use.* Business card design guidelines include:

- Standard business card size: 3.5" x 2": round or unusually shaped and sized cards can be eye-catchers, but typically they're thrown away because they're not conveniently stored

- Font type and size should be clean and easily read: 10 and 12 point, and Courier are classic; no more than two font sizes should be used; your name may be bolded and in the larger font, and the other info in the smaller font

- Colors should contrast, yet be complimentary: white with dark blue letters works well on Side 1, especially if you're using a photo; and dark blue with white letters works on Side 2

- Card-stock matters: it doesn't have to be the highest quality, but it shouldn't be paper-thin. No gimmicky glossy or highly textured card-stock: you can't write on it!

- Business cards can easily be affordable: they can be made with templates and card-stock kits from a stationary store, or purchased online at prices as low as 500 for $10

Front

Trace Duncan

Duke University
Sophomore - Marketing

+1 333..444.5555
TraceDuncan2@gmail.com
@traceduncan
www.linkedin.com/traceduncan

Career Goal

To complete a Marketing Degree that will enable me to develop a career in the public relations with a major firm sports marketing firm

Back

Trace Duncan

Duke University
Sophomore - Marketing

Skills and Accomplishments

- Strong verbal and written communications
- Completed marketing internship with a not-for-profit freshman summer
- Dean's List Student

Carry your business cards with you 100% of the time; they easily fit into your wallet or phone case. When you least expect it, you may meet someone who works in the field you're pursuing, and who you want to introduce yourself and your skills to. If you're at the gym or at a family wedding you probably aren't carrying your resume - but you can easily carry and hand out your business card.

Combined with your 30-second elevator speech, your business cards can open doors to your ideal internship.

From the desk of the SVP Human Resources:

- Employers and other professionals will see your use of a business card as professionalism and a sign of sophistication and maturity

- While you are passing out your business card, make sure you keep and include all cards you receive in your address book

- In today's social media environment professionals use business cards they receive as an immediate reminder to connect with others via LinkedIn and other SM environments; make sure that you connect with people to whom you have given your card:

The Art, Science And Importance Of Interview Preparation

Marvism

Believe it or not the majority of interviewers have limited experience interviewing and generally are not sure what they will ask when the interview begins.

Interviewing is an art and a science built on mastering skills that allow you to quickly and concisely respond to questions. The science of the interview process is understanding the proper content of expected answers. The art is the comfort level and manner in which you provide responses to questions. Your success depends upon both the science and art of interacting with a prospective employer.

The biggest problem anyone has in interviewing is the presumption that the interviewer is the world's leading expert on the topic and that the interviewer is in control of the process and in control of you. My philosophy is that if you are adequately prepared the control in the interview will become balanced. The interviewer will transition from pure evaluation of your resume and answers to a listening mode and a conversational tone. When this point is achieved, you become accomplished at the skill of interviewing.

Improving your interview skills will not be accomplished by merely reading this book. It takes work and practice. The practice will lead to confidence – the confidence will lead to success.

10 Impact Zone Steps to Successful Interviewing:

1. **Convey Who You Are:** Your 30-second elevator speech will most likely be the answer to the first question of the interview. The most experienced interviewers will normally ask, "Can you tell a little about yourself." Your preparation should include developing a list of logical questions and answers that you think will be asked. Your answers should be short, concise and to the point. Do not over explain.

2. **Learn to Explain Why Your Knowledge, Skills, Abilities and Talents Are Relevant to the Company:** Regardless of your level in any organization, the company wants to know what you will bring to the party. **Note:** *I don't mean*

*what beer. **Be prepared to provide a strong statement of what you will contribute to the organization in support of its business strategy.*** The general strategy, vision and mission of a company can always be found on the company's website. Your job is to figure out how you can help the company achieve their goals and communicate this to your potential employer.

3. **Describe Your Strengths:** Each of us has interpersonal, technical or professional assets that are of value. When asked the question, what is your greatest strength; there should be no hesitation. Not everyone is a confident speaker, particularly in stressful situations. If necessary, have notes outlining answers to likely questions written down for easy quick reference. Try not to read answers: These notes are quick, easy references. This is not embarrassing: It's smart job preparation.

4. **Describe Your Greatest Improvement Opportunity:** Describing our greatest improvement opportunity or our greatest weakness is always intimidating. Let's get one thing straight – you and I are not perfect. We each have strengths and weaknesses. The question is not to define your weaknesses. The question is designed to challenge your integrity, self-awareness and self-confidence. Often I have heard candidates answer to this question with, "My greatest weakness is that I have high standards for myself and I'm hard on myself." From my perspective, this is a weak, cop-out answer. When I am asked this question, I normally say this; *"My greatest improvement opportunity is to always be sure to listen to questions asked of me and to be concise and to the point in responding. When I do this, people realize that I am paying attention and I am sensitive to their needs and expectations."* An answer such as this not only describes the opportunity but it also describes that I am practicing and sensitive to the issue that I have just described.

5. **Learn the Most Frequently Asked Questions:** Interviewers typically ask a variety of general questions to intern candidates and those applying for entry-level jobs. These questions will likely focus on your education, experience, extracurricular activities and applicability of your knowledge, skills, abilities and talents for the job to which you are applying or to the internship that you have proposed. Be prepared. Practice the answers to these questions. Don't be afraid to rephrase the question as part of your answer, positioning the answer to emphasize your strengths. When appropriate and possible, quantify your successes using statistics, dollars, figures and percentages or simple examples, such as:

    a. The project that I completed in my last internship resulted in assisting the organization increase membership by 3%

b.   I completed my project in a 4-week period, 2-weeks ahead of schedule

c.   I was given a budget of $1,000 to organize and host the event, but I completed the project $200 under budget

6.   **Learn to Demonstrate Your Knowledge of the Company, Its People and Its Environment:** Learn as much as you can about the company and its people and its environment. This information is easily accessible through the Internet. If possible, also contact appropriate referral sources. Use what you've learned to determine whether you'd like to work for the company. Then, during the interview, mention what you have learned about the company's products and services as a springboard to an in-depth conversation.

7.   **Be Proactive With the Interviewer:** The art of interviewing is the art of engaging in a professional discussion. This conversation is focused on you but also it involves your insightfulness and interest in the company. Develop a list of thoughtful, probing questions to ask the interviewer. The level of questions will reflect your own depth of understanding of the company and what's important to you. The following is a list of questions you might ask during your interview. Remember: try to make the interview a dialogue – a 2-way conversation. You do not have to wait until the end of the interview to ask questions.

a.   In looking at my internship proposal, how would you want to measure my level of performance and success?

b.   In my research on your company, I found your corporate values to be intriguing. How did the company decide these values? (Be ready to mention several of these values to the interviewer.)

c.   I think that I am a very proactive, self-starter. But I understand and appreciate that all companies are different in how work is assigned and evaluated. What are your expectations in monitoring my work performance? I want to do a good job.

d.   I realize that you have had other interns before me. What type of people are a good fit for your company?

8.   **Stay on Point:** A major weakness for young interviewers is the inability to stay focused and on point in your answers. Focus on major points you want to communicate, and stay on point. However, you have to be nimble and flexible and think fast to adapt to questions and comments offered by the hiring manager.

9. **Game Day – Be Prepared – Mentally and Physically:** In sports, we often hear the adage, "Be prepared mentally and physically." This applies to your interview as well.

    a.   48-hours prior to your interview send a short email to the hiring manager confirming your interview, and saying that you're looking forward to your meeting

    b.   Get a good night's sleep. You can skip the off-campus party tonight and get to bed a bit early

    c.   Eat a light meal the day of interview

    d.   Dress for success – professional, yet appropriate for your age. Please, light on the cologne and perfume

    e.   Carry a small, easy access portfolio or bag, at least 2 pens and notepaper

    f.   List the questions and key points you desire to reference

    g.   Arrive a minimum of 15-minutes early for your interview - **Note:** Go to the bathroom before you arrive

    h.   Do not bring your latte or bottle of water to your interview – this isn't a casual conversation, but it's ok to accept water when offered

    i.   Turn your phone off and put it away. No quick checks of missed calls

    j.   Sometimes interviews run late, and you are left waiting in the lobby for your appointment. It's ok to check your phone for messages. It is NOT OK to wear headphones to listen to music. You don't want the interviewer calling your name repeatedly - and you can't hear

    k.   Remember, greet the receptionist and any administrative staff with courtesy and professionally - Note: I have always depended on my administrative staff to provide what I call "waiting room feedback" on candidates

10. **Game Day – Don't Eat The Donuts:** My son, MC, tells the story of a candidate for a position who had to wait for an interview. While waiting, the candidate was offered coffee and donuts sitting on a table across the room. The candidate proceeded to not only have a coffee and donut but ended up eating three donuts. As he was consuming the third jelly donut covered with

powdered sugar, the hiring manager arrived. The moral of the story – Powdered sugar, jelly filled donuts and interviews don't mix. He didn't get the job!

Social Recruiting is the evolving practice of using online social tools to recruit, interview and even hire interns and employees. Most companies use very basic social recruiting tools - like researching applicants' social media accounts for questionable statements or behaviors, or posting jobs on recruiting job sites like Simply Hired or CareerBuilder. But over 80% of companies say they are now using some form of social recruiting. Companies are beginning to experiment with social networks to advertise for open internships or jobs - often through LinkedIn, Twitter or Facebook, or Skype interviews. But tech-savvy companies have taken social recruiting to the next stage, including:

- Conducting Twitter interviews

- Hiring virtual interns

- Evaluating social media job candidates based on their Klout score or number of followers

- Targeting desired candidates via Twitter, LinkedIn or Facebook Graph Search

From the desk of the SVP Human Resources:

- The interview has been and will always be the ultimate test of your ability to perform under pressure.

- Employers want to hear your answers to questions but equally important they want to have a conversation with you in an effort to see how you engage in a professional conversation

- When possible, it's a good idea to make a "test run" of your interview. For example, you may live in the suburbs and the internship is in the city. A few days before your interview, take the train downtown, walk to the interview offices, see how people are dressed. If this is possible, it removes a lot of unknowns from the actual interview day, and helps eliminate unnecessary worries about timetables and getting lost, and how people dress for work in the city and at your potential new office

Available Online Resources:

- http://career-advice.monster.com/job-interview/intervi jobs.aspx

- http://www.askmen.com/money/career/5.html

- http://jobsearch.about.com/od/college-interviews/a/college-interview-tips.htm

- http://jobsearch.about.com/od/student/student-interview-tips.htm

- http://www.usatodayeducate.com/staging/index.php/career/three-interview-tips-every-college-student-needs-to-know

- http://www.youtube.com/watch?v=hn8Ib44GIxQ

INTERN IMPACT ZONE 12

Dressing To Create Impact

You've heard the phrase, "Dress for Success" or "Dress to Impress." My philosophy is to "Dress to Create a Positive Impact on the People Who Will Make the Decision to Hire You." The most important thing to remember is that you will never know if how you dress created a negative impression on a potential hiring manager. For this reason dressing to create a positive impact requires dressing simply and basically, with no flash or attire to draw water cooler comments after you leave. Unless, of course, your internship is for the fashion industry; in that case dress like your potential colleagues, with style and creativity - within reason.

Case Study

As the SVP of HR for a large corporation, I was returning from a meeting one day and walked back into the reception area for my department. An attractive young woman was sitting in the waiting area. I also noticed that she was dressed far too casually: high heels and a mini-skirt, and a plunging neckline. Her hair was long and she wore too much makeup. I said hello to her and others as I did anytime I passed through our lobby and waiting area. In my office, I called the receptionist.

"Who is that young woman?" I asked.

The receptionist told me the woman was there for a job interview with one of our senior recruiters. We were always looking to hire nurse practitioners – a nurse who can do many of the duties that were once confined to doctors only. On paper, this young woman had been a strong candidate for this very difficult, demanding, and responsible position.

"Do me a favor," I told the recruiter. "Please talk to her. Tell her that we are familiar with her employment and school and training records. She is a very strong candidate, which is why we asked her to come in for an interview. But tell her that the SVP of Human Resources saw her sitting there, and was struck by how inappropriately she is dressed. Give her some idea of how a person who is interviewing for such an important and responsible job should dress, and reschedule the interview."

The recruiter carried out her mission tactfully. The young woman was surprised and embarrassed. She had limited experience interviewing in the professional world. She was simply trying to look her best. She was also grateful to the recruiter. When she came in for an interview a couple of days later, she was still beautiful, but dressed in a professional yet stylish manner. The recruiter didn't comment about her appearance a couple of days earlier, or being sent home without an interview. When the interview was almost over and we indicated that a job offer would be forthcoming, she was asked if she had any more questions.

She smiled said, "No, I just want to say thank you for giving me another chance. I went home and looked at myself in mirror and this time I saw what you saw. I don't know what I was thinking."

She is now a strong employee, and a strong nurse practitioner, a leader in her department. Her story is a terrific example of the importance of dressing appropriately for an interview. She survived this faux pas only because her skills on paper were superior and we gave her the benefit of doubt and a second chance. Getting a second chance in these situations is normally unlikely. Even in creative fields like film or art, intern applicants need a shirt and tie!

Marvism

You Only Have One Chance to Make a First Impression...
Use it wisely

Men's Dress for Impact Guidelines

- As an intern, you are not expected to have an extensive wardrobe. In a formal corporate environment, one solid navy or a solid dark gray suit is sufficient. Avoid a double-breasted suit. In more casual office environments, a sports coat, dress slacks, shirt and tie are appropriate. Make sure the fabric is appropriate for all seasons and the suit and shirt clean and properly pressed.

- Blue dress shirts are great but you should avoid solid white shirts. They stain easily and can be too formal. A white shirt with a light pinstripe will also work well. Shirts should have a simple shirt collar, such as a traditional straight point, or you can use a button-down style, but avoid trendy collars and prints. In a casual work environment everyday dress may be a polo shirt and khakis, but for an interview make a good 1st impression: dress up, not down. Your effort will be noticed.

- Ties should coordinate with your suit. Reds, yellows and blues with a stripe are appropriate and support your personal style. But please, no novelty ties or crazy prints.

- For a second or third interview, simply wear a different shirt and tie.

- Your shoes should be in good repair, clean and polished. Dark simple shoes are best (black, dark brown or cordovan). Gym shoes are not a good idea for an interview unless the internship is out of doors, working with children, or some other very casual environment.

- Trim and clean your nails, comb your hair and leave your cologne for your date later in the evening.

- Use a simple briefcase or portfolio or backpack - no sports logos or bumper stickers.

Remember - it's far better to be dressed too formally for an interview than too casually.

Women's Dress for Impact Guidelines

- Black or darker color pantsuits or dress suits or dresses are appropriate for formal corporate environments like law offices or banks. Dark slacks or skirt, complimented with a blazer or sweater also works well for women. Match these items with an appropriate blouse to complete the outfit. Note: consider the length of your skirt or dress, making sure the hem is not more than three inches above the knee - try sitting down in front of a mirror to see how high a skirt creeps up when you're seated. Pay attention to slits in dresses and skirts and to necklines and buttons - no peek-a-boos.

- Shoes with heels or flats work equally well but not stilettos. Conservative offices typically require hose or tights with skirts. Offices that are more casual may not require hose, but in many cities open-toe shoes and sandals are not considered professional. This is where a test- run becomes very useful: you can see 1st hand what your colleagues are wearing.

- Your hair should be neat, your nails trimmed, and your jewelry minimal. No clanging bracelets or oversized dangling earrings.

- Use a simple briefcase or portfolio or backpack, no sports logos or stickers or dangling key chains.

- As I said to the guys, save your perfume for your date that evening

For Men and Women:

- Interviewers don't want to see any of your underwear or your tattoos, So dress like an adult, not a kid. A business guideline for appropriate work attire is to dress for the job you want, not the one you have: meaning even if your job is in the mailroom, dress like you have an office in the C-suite. Over simplified, but you get it!

- Finally, it may sound basic but please brush your teeth, take a shower and use deodorant! Keep a breath mint in your briefcase and put it in just before your interview. You don't know how your competition will do, so give yourself every advantage.

From the desk of the SVP Human Resources:

- No matter if the place you are interviewing is a business casual company, or a Wall Street firm never be so presumptuous to not appear for your interview in anything but professional attire

- Employers expect you to dress for the job want

Available Online Resources

- http://career-advice.monster.com/job-interview/interview-appearance/dress-for-success/article.aspx

- http://jobsearch.about.com/od/interviewattire/a/interviewdress.htm

- http://www.davidsonstaffing.com/articles/dress-code.aspx

INTERN IMPACT ZONE 13

Demonstrating Social Maturity, Clean Up Your Act

Employers are also online!

The television show *The Job* featured Cosmopolitan Magazine Editor-in-Chief, Joanna Coles interviewing finalists for an Assistant Editor position. The final question posed to the two finalists, was "Is there anything in your social media accounts that would be embarrassing to you, your family and most importantly to Cosmopolitan?" You could see the candidate's mind spinning, asking themselves the question, "What's out there that I don't remember?" *Social maturity is an absolute must.* The vast majority of students are social media savvy but socially immature and naive in understanding the liability that their social media behaviors will have. The following points are a minimum prerequisite to your online job search success. I am not going to argue the issues. I am going to tell you bluntly the reality and rules of demonstrating Social Maturity. First and foremost, remember:

Marvism

Your social media behaviors are Permanent Actions that will be seen by others and used to determine if you will get a job!

Social Media (SM):

Your behavior on Facebook, Twitter, Pinterest, Instagram, Snap Chat, LinkedIn and every other social media outlet matters.

While there is ample discussion about the legality of prospective employers probing your social media sites and demanding access, the central question is which of your actions will place you in a potential situation where immature behaviors will be a barrier to your career success.

There are many ways to share privately with your friends - begin to view your name and image as professional territory and beware that anyone and everyone has access to your social media thoughts, photos and behaviors.

Social Media Action Items:

- Any social media site with your name attached should be immediately cleared of any questionable material. This includes questionable language and images of you and your friends

- Check your privacy settings: Remember when you check-in to a bar on Facebook and post it to Twitter a potential employer may question why a 20 year old is in a bar - and why they advertised it

- Ask friends to refrain from tagging or linking you to questionable material. You may not share photos, but your friends might post photos and tag you in these photos

- Consider creating a social media account with a name that your friends can easily link to you, but does not link to your real name. Ok, I get it, you are young and stuff happens. Just be smart and project your SM identity if you and your friends decide to go crazy one night

- Create a professional LinkedIn Profile that contains the following:

  - Professional/Business Photo, different from a Facebook "personality" photo

  - Current resume

  - Professional objective: a work internship

  - Work, internship and volunteer experience

  - School courses relevant to your career goals

  - Social and professional interests, affiliations and rewards

  - Skills and personal interests such as: 6 years French and enjoys European travel

  Note: Separate this Professional Page from your Personal Facebook Page or from your Twitter activities designed for your friends, followers and fans. Just because you have a Twitter account doesn't mean you have to advertise it on LinkedIn. Beware of flashback from comments on political, social and religious SM commentary

- Insure you have completed a comprehensive biographical summary. Examples:

  - Junior, University of Michigan, computer science major searching for a Fall 2014 internship in Pittsburgh, PA.

  - Graduating, Indiana University, Business Accounting Major seeking a full-time permanent position or internship to gain experience and to begin a career in a financial services environment

- A sophomore, medical science major from Stanford University seeking summer 2013 internship opportunity in a healthcare environment

- Link with as many friends, family and professional acquaintances as you can

- Create a short, professional LinkedIn connect request note. The following is sample:

  "Hello Mr. or Ms. XYZ,

  I am a senior at the University of Notre Dame. As I complete my education, I am beginning to expand my professional network. I would appreciate connecting with you to learn and expand my professional knowledge. Thank you for your time and I look forward to hearing from you.

  Sincerely,

  Jane"

The following is a list of connections whom you should contact and actions you should regularly engage within LinkedIn:

- Link with alumni and professors from your university

- Link with as many family and friends as possible

- Research companies of interest and follow these companies

- Research and join LinkedIn Groups representing alumni and your career interest. Remember you can join up to 50 groups

- Connect with members of your LinkedIn Groups that mirror your career interests, skills, personal hobbies and extracurricular activities

- Request recommendations and endorsements from people who can attest to your skills

- Update your biographical summary as often as needed, at least monthly – remember these updates are posted to your connections, keeping your face and name in front of potential employers or referrals

- Again, remember that employers are also online – If there is something in your Social Media that you don't want mom and dad to see, an employer doesn't want to see it either

Anecdote

My wife was recently contacted via LinkedIn by a current student from her Notre Dame LinkedIn Women's Alumni Group, asking for help in landing a marketing internship. My wife replied, asking the student to specify:

- What type of internship

- Where she wanted to work

- When she wanted to do the internship

After the response from the student, who also sent a LI connect request, my wife replied she didn't have contacts in that city, but made some general suggestions on finding an opportunity including being specific in her request for help. She advised her not to discourage a prospective employer by not providing important details of your request for help– be prepared with all the details. Remember, employers are busy and may not have the time or inclination to probe. She also informed the student there were several typos in her original email.

From the Desk of the SVP Human Resources:

- There is never an occasion when an employer will not do at least a quick internet search on you

- There are several tools to help you analyze and sanitize your online profile, like Google Alerts, Social Alerts, Reppler or Qnary.

- *"Grammarly Lite"* is a free tool for identifying your online spelling and grammatical errors

Available Online Resources:

- http://blogs.hbr.org/cs/2012/05/the_new_professional.html#.T6r6nEs 3GCk.googlehttp://

INTERN IMPACT ZONE 14

Intern Impact Through Networking

Very few people actually enjoy networking. But for almost everyone, networking is critical to landing a job. Your university probably organizes job fairs and internship fairs, where you sign-up to meet prospective internship providers and pitch them on how your skills and talents are exactly what their business needs.

But there are many other networking opportunities that can assist your internship search:

1. University alumni networking events: these may be on-campus, or regional events near your hometown. Look on your school website for alumni activities.

2. LinkedIn group meet-ups and networking events: many professional groups hold local events for members to meet, socialize, and exchange professional tips.

3. Community classes and workshops: many towns, schools, and community groups sponsor free and low-fee classes to develop professional and recreational skills, such as public speaking, foreign language, cooking, social media, or computer skills. Taking - or teaching - these classes are ideal opportunities to meet small business owners who might offer you an ideal internship opportunity.

4. Many churches hold social hours for members to meet and socialize.

5. Search for free lectures, book signings, or other appearances near or on-campus or at home on break with leaders in your field. You might have a chance to talk to the presenter: but you'll definitely have an opportunity to talk to other attendees, who have interests similar to yours and just might have an internship opportunity!

6. Social networking is networking. Many online groups have Twitter chats, open forums, hangouts, call-in webinars, Q&A sessions and other online events where you can meet professionals in your field. After all, *if internships can be virtual, networking can be virtual!*

Learning to network in this millennium is very important and a tool that all professionals use. Here a few tips from the Intern Impact Zone on networking:

*   Hand out your business card: but always ask for theirs! Then when you get home you can contact them with your info and remind them of your meeting, not sit at home and wait for them to call you

- Carry a pen so you can write a quick note on their business card, such as '89 grad UM, played on tennis team

- Be prepared to give your 30-second elevator speech and to listen to theirs! Not only will you get valuable information on your new contacts, you'll also get tips for perfecting your pitch

- Think of a conversation opener - other than your elevator speech. If you have the opportunity to continue your conversation, don't fumble for a topic. Ask questions. Show interest, remember you're learning and you're selling yourself, your skills, talents and potential. Mention the new biography you just read, or your trip to Europe, or your schools' big game last weekend: Look for a topic that you're comfortable discussing, but is also an easy start to casual conversation.

- Quality, not quantity counts: This is not a speed-dating event. Of course the more people you connect with, the higher your chance of meeting someone who can assist your career goals. But if the first person you talk to is in your field, is interested in you and your career, and you enjoy talking to them don't feel pressure to meet more people. One quality contact is worth far more than 15 fast business card exchanges

- Never be uncomfortable or shy at a network event, remember, just like you, everyone is at the networking event to make new contacts

From the desk of the SVP Human Resources:

- Anyone can network: Not everyone gets good results by networking!

- Professionals use every social occasion as an opportunity to network

- Never leave home without a stack of business cards with you, the key to networking is the 30 Second Elevator Speech and an exchange of Business Cards

Available Online Resources:

- http://www.careerkey.org/asp/career_development/networking.html

- http://www.cio.com/article/164300/How_to_Network_12_Tips_for_Shy_People

- http://www.rileyguide.com/network.html

INTERN IMPACT ZONE 15

International Internships: Finding Opportunities Around the World

The world is a big place and the global market place is ever expanding!

If you're majoring in a field that would benefit from experience abroad there are internship opportunities for you. However, it takes a person willing to accept the challenges and barriers of expatriate life. Living and working in a foreign country sounds exciting and is a wonderful opportunity to see the world. However, living and working abroad is not the same as a summer vacation in Europe. It takes additional planning, some unique resources and a willingness to think and work differently than in America.

I lived and worked in other countries for nearly 10 years and I've traveled and worked in nearly 30 countries. As an HR executive I was able to hire a number of Americans in these companies as interns, as well as hire local country students for internships. In my expat experiences, I have worked with other Americans in the expat community whose children found internship opportunities for global companies. My experiences were amazing and fulfilling, and I grew tremendously on an interpersonal and professional level, made valuable contacts, and expanded my career opportunities. **This is the goal of any internship, whatever the country.**

In this chapter I focus on two international internship populations:

- Children of Expats: desiring to find internships while living abroad

- US University Students: desiring to find internships abroad

Children of Expats

Expat life is a major challenge for the entire family, but teenage students have challenges unique to the change in culture – and often language - and the differences in their educational environment. Despite these differences and challenges, expat students can experience a unique opportunity for internships within foreign companies.

Stage, apprenticeship, praktikum, practicas profesionales, work experience, sandwich placement: in any language, an internship is a paid or unpaid, on-the-job learning opportunity, sometimes for college credit. But the practices and laws governing internships vary greatly from country to country, so it is critical that students NOT make assumptions based on their home country's laws, but work closely with their university or employer to be sure they are in compliance.

Here are some useful tips, ideas and resources that students and parents can use to assist expat students gain valuable professional experience while abroad:

1.   As part of the parents' expat package, propose to the host company an unpaid work experience for your child, or recommend other companies where a work experience may be possible.

2.   If your child will be a attending university in a foreign country, internships are now a standard part of the curriculum.

3.   In many European universities, internships are often designed as team projects required for school credit.

4.   As in the US, a resume (aka in Europe "CV") will be required, however the standards for resume writing do vary from country to country. Therefore, some online research will be required. Your university and local HR department will be able to provide examples.

American University Students:

As part of the university experience, many American college students want to take a semester abroad, or an internship abroad. Time, planning and preparation are key to finding a good international internship. There are many online resources available to assist you in finding an internship or work-study abroad. In addition to your college's internship or career department, see the career departments for other universities; you may be able to find an internship through their program. Note: when working with most international internship programs and companies, the intern pays a fee for this internship opportunity. Be careful and thorough in your research so that you fully understand all fees, restrictions and waivers so that you don't end up paying more than you planned for far less than you need, particularly with online programs based in other countries.

Philip Berry, President of Philip Berry Associates LLC, a global management-consulting firm, has lived and worked in over 60 countries and gained extensive experience in human capital improvement strategies on a global level. In his work with major global corporations such as Colgate-Palmolive and Proctor Gamble, Philip has worked extensively with global internship programs, "I have worked with and developed international internship programs and interns from around the world. In my time working in both the US and while on assignment in Latin America and

Europe we recruited student interns from around the world including: Africa, Asia, Europe, Latin America and of course the US. Our goal was always to develop a program that grew a global talent base for the company. The author of the book *"Being Better Than You Believe: 8 Steps to Ultimate Success,"* Philip stated, "Our interns were diverse and represented functions such as: marketing, finance, IT, supply chain management and human resources. They came from schools around the world, mostly focused on graduate programs such as INSEAD, Thunderbird, Cambridge, Columbia and NYU."

Philip like other human capital development experts, emphasizes the importance that interns understand the magnitude of these opportunities, "Just like in the US internship opportunities are highly competitive. If you get the opportunity you have to use it to your greatest advantage." Philip noted several points, "First, you have to understand that this is a job and we are evaluating your performance just like we evaluate our regular employees. You find a way to impact the organization as an individual, but at the same time demonstrate global teamwork and an ability to work in complex work environments. Second, I always advise our students to network with everyone in the company, get to know as many people as you can and allow them to get to know you. The last point I would make is that companies are always looking for global talent and this is your opportunity to grow and demonstrate your ability to contribute to the success of the organization. In the end it is our goal to hire the best of best."

Before going further into understanding how to search for an internship position abroad, you need to ask yourself a few questions:

1. What experience have you had traveling abroad?

2. What are your language skills?

3. Are you a flexible person and willing to deal with change?

4. List the countries where you have an interest in working.

5. For each country you have listed, research a list of work issues that you must consider.

    a. Governmental rules, regulations and qualifications, including passport and visa requirements

    b. Language skills

    c. Gender issues

After answering these questions, you have a basis to understand if your expectations are reasonable and whether you have the basic requirements to pursue opportunities.

Your search for internships abroad is not a great deal different than searching for opportunities in the USA. The following recommendations will assist you in your target company search:

1. Conduct an Internet search of the following types of companies:

    a. US owned companies with global operations in the countries you want to consider

    b. Foreign owned companies with operations in the US

    c. Foreign owned companies located exclusively outside of the US

2. Your university placement office will have resources and contacts available for international internships. Start early, international internships are highly competitive.

3. LinkedIn Jobs has extensive listings for internships, many of them international opportunities.

4. Sending your resume/CV to headhunters and agencies, writing open application letters, and responding to ads in the newspapers are also viable sources in Europe.

5. Your ability to attain a tourist, student or work visa in your targeted country will be your major barrier, some companies will be willing to sponsor you, but be prepared. There is a cost and hard-work in getting your visa. Different countries have differing visa and internship rules, so research is critical to determining what those rules are.

6. The CIEE and BUNACC Work Abroad exchanges enable students to secure work permits in advance, then look for a job on-site with assistance from overseas offices.

7. A US-based company InterExchange is a 40 year old, non-profit specializing in cultural exchange experience that also supports the placement of interns around the world.

8. Attempt to match your targeted search to your global skills and skills that might be desirable to a specific company – Example: a person who has studied

French for 5 years and has traveled in Europe extensively is likely to have more success in French companies.

9. Develop a specific resume/CV to highlight your global skills and interests – however, the standards for resume writing are unique to various countries, therefore, some research will be required.

10. Develop your proposal under the same country-specific format.

11. Develop your Letter of Introduction with emphasis on your previous work and internship experiences and skills that specify what you can contribute to non-US work environment.

Case Study: An Internship from China: Lesson in Life and Internships

Drew Tilson is an Emerging Markets specialist who has lived and worked in both China and India. He speaks fluent Mandarin and is a multicultural expert. The story he tells of international internships is one of humor but caution when working in less modern, advanced environments.

I was working in an education environment in China and I had a student studying hospitality management. I was having a tough day, and he had come over to visit. He said, "I know you're busy right now, but maybe telling you about my summer internship will give you a laugh and put things in perspective."

He went on to tell me how he had contracted with a local headhunter to get a summer internship. The headhunter had set him up with a local hotel in the city of Zhengzhou. He showed up with a group of students for the first day of work, but the hotel did not have enough rooms set aside for the students. They set several students up on the roof till they could set aside more rooms...the first night... it rained. They got soaked. They finally got them set up the next day - crammed lots of kids per room. To say the least this would not go over well in the US.

The job...let's just say it was not the most positive in the world. The hotel assigned him to introduce customers to pretty massage ladies in the spa. I think you get the idea. Even worse, he had to clean up after massages as well :(

To top it off, the third party headhunter took off with the money and the interns did not see a dime for their summer work. The intern finished by saying... "I hope you don't feel your day is worse than my summer internship." He was so right - I could not really compare to that, and I was a bit amused by the terrible circumstances that some of the students would endure all for the sake of an internship and experience.

Drew's advice to Interns:

This story, while humorous at one level is very sad and gives a clear message that with international internships you must be careful with who you contract for the job. I would say that where so many internships are lacking - not just in China and India, but in the US as well. Practical experience is the key. Practical real world application that makes education come alive and able to be applied - the real-world skills that graduates will need to secure jobs and demonstrate hard skills to set them apart from other candidates. I would say this has been the biggest shift from when I was in school like so many other things, recruiting kids in grade school for major college sports, internships have shifted way down the ladder as jobs become more and more competitive. It was a junior and senior year in college idea to have an internship, now the world is shifting more towards freshman and sophomore year.

It also is common for high school students to have internships to get into the best colleges. While in high school they can demonstrate the skills colleges expect you have for success.

From the desk of the SVP Human Resources:

- International internships require additional knowledge, skills, abilities and resources to insure success

Available Company and Online Resources:

The following companies and online resources offer assistance for finding international internships. I have not worked with any of these companies, nor can I vouch for any of them: As stated above, do your research so you're thoroughly aware of any fees, restrictions and requirements:

- Interexchange, Inc.: 161 Sixth Avenue, New York, NY 10013, USA. Tel. 212-924-0446; toll-free 1.800.597.3675. Email: info@interexchange.org Website: www.InterExchange.org

- American Medical Student Association: http://www.amsa.org/AMSA/ Homepage.aspx

- Institute of International Education: http://www.iie.org/fulbright

- US Department of State: http://www.state.gov

- Univ. of Michigan, International Center's Overseas Opportunities Office: internationalcenter.umich.edu/swt/

- Global Experiences: http://www.globalexperiences.com/students/internships.php

- Simply Hired: http://www.simplyhired.com/a/jobs/list/q-internships

- Global Placement.com: http://www.globalplacement.com/

- TransitionsAbroad.com: http://www.transitionsabroad.com/listings/work/internships/articles/internationinternships.shtml

- Abroad Internship: http://www.facebook.com/pages/Abroad-Internship-Find-Paid-International-Internships/242630083956

- Women in Progress: http://womeninprogress.org/student/internships.asp?gclid=COKP5qPw4LUCFQ-xnQodxlYAEg

- Go Abroad: http://www.goabroad.com/intern-abroad

Other Resources:

- How To Pursue An International Internship from University of Pennsylvania Career Services: http://www.vpul.upenn.edu/careerservices/international-internships.html

- AIESEC: http://www.aiesec.org/cms/aiesec/AI/students/International_Internship. html

- International Internships: http://www.international-internships.com

- Oversees Internships Can Benefit, For a Price: http://www.nytimes.com/2012/03/25/jobs/workstation-overseas-internships-can-benefit-for-a-price.html?_r=0

Case Study: Organizational Development Internship

Goals:

- Find a team-based internship in a global French-based corporation that allows a team of MBA students to develop, implement and complete an international organizational development project

Miriam, Helka and Liza were required as the final element of their MBA at HEC, France's leading business school, to complete an organizational development project. Miriam was French, Helka came from Switzerland and Liza was American. The three girls approached me as the Chief Learning Officer of Pechiney SA, a multinational materials fabricator and packaging corporation, for an opportunity to development a pilot global training program. The team reported to the Director of Organizational Development. This internship project was designed for a 6-months in duration. The 2 non-French women were eligible to work with the company based on student visas granted through the university. The team developed the following course for their project:

Project Summary

The agreed on subject was to develop a 3-day workshop intended as a "train-the-trainer" program for Human Resources professionals in various countries around the world. The course focused on HR trainers who had limited experience in presenting a course on basic supervisory skills.

Project Objectives:

- The design of this course aimed to provide new supervisors skills needed for success

- Set up a training plan to use for the course

- Work with Subject Matter Experts and managers to determine course content

- Analyze level and experience of learners to target the course accurately

- Determine constraints and restrictions affecting the course – including time and budgeting issues

- Conduct task analysis to determine course content

Design tests and exercises

- Apply principles of adult learning in the course

- Develop course materials such as handouts and practice exercises

The project served to provide the 3 interns a broad-based understanding of the following:

- Techniques for understanding customer requirements

- Estimating design time of future projects

- Reducing course costs and length

- Assuring job relevance of the course

- Developing course content

- Linking learning to job experience

- Writing clear objectives

- Testing

- How to develop and use job aids and materials

Upon the conclusion of the project I required the 3 interns to present to senior HR professionals and the SVP HR a complete written and verbal summary of the program developed. Due to the success of project and skills demonstrated, Miriam and Liza were offered positions in the company as trainers for the course they developed. Helka was successful in securing a position within her home country.

Lessons Learned:

- While all 3 women were multilingual as requirement of attending HEC, each realized the importance of being multicultural in implementing programs in a global business environment, noting a need to resolve cultural conflicts amongst themselves in how they each approach the work process

- They realized that various cultures received their work at different levels, feeling that interns were too inexperienced to develop such a course with some professionals questioning the experience needed to develop such a program

10 Intern Impact Zone Leadership Challenges

Marvism

Never miss an opportunity – Never be afraid to fail - Never be afraid to stretch yourself to achieve success.

The following 10 questions define your opportunity to demonstrate your leadership potential.

1. How have I influenced my friends or family, teammates, classmates and others to make good verses bad decisions?

_____

_____

_____

2. How have I changed my own behavior to be a better person or professional?

_____

_____

_____

3. How have I improved myself to be a better performer and to improve outcomes?

_____

_____

_____

4. How have I motivated or inspired the performance of others to exceed their potential?

_____

_____

_____

5.   How have I sourced or discovered new resources or tools to improve environments where I have worked?

_____

_____

_____

6.   When have I interceded with family, friends, classmates or teammates to resolve conflict?

_____

_____

_____

7.   How have I contributed to the vision or growth of a company, team project or to my superiors?

_____

_____

_____

8.   How have I overcome adversity or disappointments in life?

_____

_____

_____

9.   How have I led a team or project to achieve successful completion?

_____

_____

_____

10. How has my work allowed me to grow toward my future goals?

_____

_____

_____

From the Desk of the SVP Human Resources:

- Employers look for employees who desire to make an impact on the organizations, the same applies to interns – try to find ways to impact the organization through your talents, knowledge, skills and abilities

- You must be able to communicate how you've impacted those around you

The 5 Irrefutable Laws That Will Result In Immediate Termination

Starting a job typically involves filling out forms and reviewing many HR policies and procedures. But some employment rules are so basic that they may not be in the HR Manuals. You need to know them.

1. **Violation of Internet Policy:** Your company email address and the Internet environment at the office and your assigned computer belong to the company. If you abuse it, expect to lose it - your job.

2. **Honesty, Integrity and Trust.** Making mistakes is a normal part of professional life. Not being forthright regarding errors leads to bigger problems, a lack of trust and termination.

3. **Violating Confidentiality.** All organizations expect you to maintain confidential information. Even if it is not specifically stated to you, it is assumed that you will not publicize information such as strategy, trade secrets, salary information and other proprietary information.

4. **Falsifying Your Qualifications.** Falsifying your qualifications is a sure way of being eliminated from consideration. Most companies outsource the process of verifying your qualifications.

5. **Plagiarizing Work.** If you are in college you know the sin of plagiarism. The simple rule: Don't do it!

From the desk of the SVP Human Resources:

- All organizations are very sensitive about maintaining integrity and trust. - Customers and clients holding organizations and all employees to a higher standard than ever before

- Your behaviors, decisions and actions are permanent impressions on your professional reputation

Available Online Resources:

- http://smallbusiness.chron.com/employee-consequences-breach-confidentiality-15476.html

- http://www.arsbackgrounds.com/falsified_resumes.html

- http://www.ehow.com/info_7956448_plagiarism-professional-consequences.html

- http://jobsearch.about.com/od/onlinecareernetworking/a/violating-company-social-networking-policy.htm

10 Intern Impact Zone Productivity And
High-Impact Opportunities

Once you have secured your internship, your next challenge is how to get started, how to be productive and how to make an impact. I call this *"Find Your Intern Impact Zone"* – the place where you make a difference in the organization. The following are 10 tips to help you demonstrate to the organization that you are a self-starter and a productive, eager partner in the business.

1. **Introduce yourself to as many people in the organization as possible.** Don't expect or wait for people to take you by the hand and introduce you to everyone in the office. Use your 30-second elevator speech as a basis for introducing yourself. Ask questions during these conversations. Use them as learning opportunities and to demonstrate your interest in people, what they do and how the organization operates. Remember, everyone at your new job was also once the new kid at work – demonstrate your maturity and initiative.

2. Ask your boss as part of your orientation if it is possible to **interview leaders of the organization.** These leaders enjoy talking to young, bright people and are generally willing to share thoughts and experiences when they have time. By the way, if a meeting gets cancelled, simply reschedule - don't take it personally. Things do come up for busy executives.

3. **Document a weekly, bullet point summary of the work you have completed** and present it to your supervisor. Keep this list simple and easy to read – no fluff stuff. The following is an example of the list you might submit.

    a. Completed a work plan with 10 key steps to complete my project

    b. Conducted 2 interviews with key executives

    c. Attended the new Strategy Project kickoff session

    d. I had several key learning points this week:

        i. From my executive interviews I learned how the company makes strategic decisions through a process

ii.   Learned it is important to listen to details and be willing to ask questions for clarity to be sure I understand an assignment

iii. Learned that organizations can be political and that it is important to understand how to deal with political issues

5. If not already arranged by your supervisor, **every 2-weeks ask your boss for a short meeting to discuss your progress.**

6. If you don't have work to do at any given time, **look for opportunities to assist others.** It should not be beneath your pay-grade to answer phones when a clerical professional is away from his or her desk.

7. **Never be late to work, for meetings or with deadlines.** In fact, arrive at work a little early and don't leave early at the end of your day.

1. **Practice your communication skills.** Speak clearly and succinctly. Practice active listening skills.

8. **Keep a "To Do" list.** Each day before leaving, check your list and set priorities you want to complete the next day. Arrive at work the next day knowing what you are going to work on. Try to stay on task, avoid distractions unless necessary – stuff happens.

9. **Keep a notebook with you at all times. Document your thoughts, ideas, directions given and notes from meetings.** People will notice your attention to detail and accuracy.

Marvisim

Even in this electronic era be careful using smart devices to take notes in meetings and in one- on-one interaction; it can be distracting to the people you are meeting. Remember, eye contact in meetings is important – "Are you listening to me or are you texting your mom?"

10. **Leave your social media and personal email activity for home.** Do not use the company's email, Internet, or company time for your personal use. Companies are very sensitive about this misuse.

From the desk of the SVP Human Resources:

- Finding ways to demonstrate your impact on an organization is key to any job, at any level of the organization

- Your ability to document progress and your impact on the organization will assist you demonstrating organizational skills and will keep you and work in front of the right people who are evaluating your performance

INTERN IMPACT ZONE 19

The 6 Most Important Intern Impact Zone Competencies

1. Be Ethically Grounded, Driving Integrity and Trust

Ethics, Integrity and Trust cannot be separated. Integrity is the level of moral fiber that we possess. Trust is the reward you will receive when people realize our level of integrity. Ethics are the foundation on which our integrity and trust are created.

- A direct truthful individual

- Provides the truth with professionalism

- Maintains confidences

- Acknowledges your own shortcomings

- Never misrepresents for personal gain

- Rewards the right values and challenges others to live up to values

2. Be a Relentless Communicator

The relentless communicator is one that is never satisfied until he or she is sure that you give the right messages and everyone does what you are saying and meant to say. Speak to everyone with respect and express respect for the work that is done.

- Precise, specific to the point in both verbal and written communications

- Demonstrates outstanding listening skills

3. Practice Humility and Approachability

Interns must possess a significant level of self-confidence in order to persevere against the greatest of obstacles. However, it is your humility or modesty in your own self-worth that will differentiate you. Therefore, you must practice and learn leadership as a natural element of everyday life. Your self-confidence should provide a humbleness that allows and encourages others to approach.

- Self-confidence

- Has a controlled sense of his or her own importance

- Allows others to be at ease

- Pleasant and energizing

- Sensitive and patient

4. Seek to Engage, Empower and Inspire Yourself and Others

Giving yourself and others the authority to succeed and fail is not easy. However, it is the best way for you, your teammates and the organization and its associates to grow. Further, you must learn to be a leader that understands you can empower others, you should learn to show the way through encouragement and individual development and teamwork. As an intern you should strive to inspire others.

- Provides everyone the opportunity to discuss, debate and make decisions

- Energizes and builds commitment

5. Practice Leadership Courage

You are an intern but you can also be a leader with the self-confidence to speak and contribute with authority. Willingness to engage at all levels of the organization.

- Will not hold back when a voice is needed, but speaks with professionalism and in a responsible way

- Willing to state the good and the bad

6. Continuously Searches for Impact Zone

Leaders are expected to make a significant, coordinated impact on the organization. They are expected to establish their presence in the organization and to orchestrate a symphony of business success. Colleagues and subordinates alike know who these leaders are and know their potential to change the outcome in the most crucial times.

- Finds the way to support the team

- Is not discouraged in the search for continuous improvement of self and the organization

***

This chapter on internship competency development is an excerpt from my first book **Linebacker in the Boardroom: Lessons in Life and Leadership.** This book is a discussion, advice and lessons I learned as my career evolved and grew in corporate America.

Marv

INTERN IMPACT ZONE 20

Final Lessons in Internship Leadership

No matter where you are in your career, each of us must be leaders. I don't believe that people are born leaders and leaders are not just the people at the top of the organization. Organizations search for leadership qualities at all levels of the organization. This includes interns. The basic qualities of leadership are a set of abilities that we possess and use at different times and stages of life.

- Our ability to guide

- Our ability to influence others by our actions, thoughts and ideas

- Our ability to drive direction

- Our ability to model certain behaviors

- Our ability to engage, motivate and inspire others

My first book *Linebacker in the Boardroom: Lessons in Life and Leadership* focused on the impact of my sports career and how it established the foundation for who I am today. In this book, I took the opportunity to share my stories from an inside-the-locker room look at the Notre Dame football lifestyle and how it established, developed and inspired my leadership philosophy. I attempted to provide an understanding of what it takes to persevere against the odds, and how to achieve superior performance both on and off the field. I provided ideas, thoughts and inspirations for leaders of today and tomorrow.

I offered readers my philosophy of leadership, focused on how each of us "Find the Impact Zone", the place where we use our talents and gifts and our knowledge, skills and abilities are used to make the difference in the world around. **Your internship is a first step in finding your Professional Impact Zone.** Each of us is a leader. We are not born leaders, we are developed, molded and shaped to provide our own leadership impact. Regardless of our level in any organization, whether you are a janitor, a clerical professional, CEO or an intern, we can and should demonstrate leadership in terms of our behavior and how we impact others. Leadership is not reserved for those at the top of the organization. Leadership is our essential, exceptional and ethical behaviors that others evaluate and respect.

Essential Exceptional Ethical Leadership™ is my trademarked leadership model that says:

- Leaders must be seen as **Essential** to the environment around them and they must seen as relevant and provide essential knowledge, skills and abilities to the organization; knowledge, skills and abilities are in demand and respected by everyone in the organization

- Leaders must be **Exceptional** in terms of how they perform and how they use their knowledge, skills and ability, exceeding expectations and being respected for their hard work and perseverance

- Leaders must be **Ethical** and be a model of behavior and have a moral foundation that meets the expectations of society and the environment in which they are working

Essential Exceptional Ethical Leadership™ (aka 3E Leadership) must be at the center of the work you do as an intern or in any job that you occupy.

Finally, whether you are approaching your first internship, first full-time position or in any other stage of employment, view each occasion as an opportunity to learn, mold and shape your leadership and impact on others.

From the desk of the SVP Human Resources:

- You will find in your career that all companies consistently look for those who are able and willing to lead

- Leadership is not always about those at the top of the organization, but those that step up and influence people and outcomes

Good Luck and Find Your Internship Impact Zone!

Appendix

To assist you in your internship journey this Appendix contains sample:

- Case Studies and Sample Internships

- Sample 30-Second Elevator Speeches

- Sample Internship Job Descriptions

- Sample Letters Of Introduction

- Sample LinkedIn Letters Of Introduction

- Sample Follow-Up Thank You Letters

- Sample Resumes

- Sample Performance Evaluations

- Internship Federal Guidelines

These tools are designed to help your create your ideal Internship Proposal. Together with your business card, LinkedIn profile and LI network contacts and the other advice and tools in this book, you have everything you will need to find your ideal internship and be successful on the job.

Case Studies and Sample Internships

The following are a series of real internship scenarios to provide ideas of how internships are structured and in some cases how internships are found and implemented. These students have used a wide variety of resources to find and secure their internship. They have had successes and setbacks in their efforts but most importantly, they did not accept failure as an option.

Case Study: Engineering Internship

Goals:

- Find a rewarding internship that builds upon previous work experience

- Maintain a somewhat flexible schedule that allows continuance of a tutoring commitment on campus

Katlyn is a senior chemical engineering student at Boston College. Through the cooperative education program at her school, she completed two rewarding full-time co-ops. In her sophomore year, she spent six months working with the Research Division at a small biotech company helping to develop nanoparticle vaccines and immunotherapies. Through this opportunity, Katlyn gained valuable hands-on laboratory experience as a competitively paid full-time co-op student. For her second co-op, Katlyn worked on a collaborative project with the Chemical Engineering Department at MIT and a large pharmaceutical company with aims to develop a pilot scale system for continuous drug manufacturing. This experience further developed Katlyn's background in the pharmaceutical industry and taught her additional lessons in various analytical techniques, troubleshooting and working with an interdisciplinary team. Katlyn was even able to extend this paid co-op through the summer of her third year at BC.

For the summer before her final year of study in her five-year BS/MS program at Boston College, Katlyn wanted to complete an internship that would build upon her previous experiences from her co-ops and stay within her desired niche in the pharmaceutical industry.

Katlyn was also hoping for flexibility in her schedule, as she had already committed to a tutoring job on campus that would consume about ten hours a week. She quickly realized that finding a summer-only internship that fit her specific needs was not an easy feat without the help of her school's reputable Co-op Program. After a few months of filling out online applications for nearby opportunities, Katlyn realized it was time to develop her own internship. She emailed one of her Professors on campus and set up a meeting to discuss possible projects she could work on in the Professor's Drug Delivery Research Laboratory. Her Professor was very open to the idea and helped develop the project into something that would benefit the research being done and, at the same time, fulfill Katlyn's internship desire. Because her new internship was located on campus (where her tutoring took place), she was able to accommodate both commitments. Katlyn was awarded a research grant from Boston College to fund her project and was able to turn the summer internship into a part-time job for her final two semesters at BC.

When asked what advice she would give to other students looking to gain valuable internship experience, Katlyn offered three key points:

- Be proactive in your internship search and don't hesitate to reach out to your academic and professional network for guidance when you need it

- Don't settle for something that you don't think will fit with your long-term goals

- Show your employer your best work every day and they will recognize and appreciate your commitment

- The relationships you develop during internships could be instrumental in your career and/or graduate school search

Case Study: Legal Internship

Goals:

- Complete an internship in a law firm to gain experience in how the legal industry works and the type of work lawyers do each day

- Use the internship to explore career options and gain experience in a major that compliments the work done by the legal firm

Brian is a junior business major at the University of Notre Dame. His goal is to attend law school after graduation. He completed his second internship during the summer 2012 with the legal firm of Karlin, Fleisher and Falkenberg, an Illinois-based firm. Brian's internship was focused in the area of legal research. His task was to assist the senior partner in researching the background, details, facts and statistics on cases. The research conducted included statistical analysis, which compliments Brian's accounting specialty at Notre Dame. This is Brian's second summer interning at this firm. Brian commented, "Last year I did many different things around the office, but this year the work I'm doing is tedious and detail oriented. It involves a great deal of research on actual cases. It's real life and you see the difficulties people are facing." Brian noted that his biggest concern is not to make errors, "I know I'm not perfect, but I don't want to make stupid errors. I want people to be happy I'm here. If I can't do good work the senior partner is still going to have to fix my errors. There is no one else. This is a small firm and very hands-on."

Jon Fleisher, a senior partner at the firm, says Brian's work is real research, "At first you're cautious about the types of work that we give interns. We need to understand their limits and their commitment to doing high quality work." Jon said when Brian is not here, "We have do this work ourselves, so he truly adds value, but it takes time to teach the tools, techniques and rules of the game." This law firm has used legal interns for a number of years. They learned how to maximize the benefits for both the intern and the firm. Jon noted that training and follow up are important elements to the program, "The more effort we place on teaching the right skills, the better the intern becomes. We always hope our internships result in full-time permanent opportunities. This is a learning opportunity, but there are no guarantees. All of the lawyers here have had internship experience, so we recognize the difficulties these young students face."

As Brian enters the second semester of his junior year, he is studying in London. Upon his return he will once again look to secure an internship for the summer. He may attempt to expand his options this year, considering an internship in his undergraduate field of accounting. His thought is that working in an accounting firm is a logical experience where his undergraduate major could be combined with his experience over the last two summers in the law firm. If he decides to go to law school, Brian will have a head start on others entering the field. Brian's experience is an excellent example of how internships should be used to test drive potential career choices, gain experience in your discipline and make money during the summer. More importantly, this case demonstrates that internships are not just about doing grunt work.

Jon offered several recommendations to those seeking internships:

1.   When you are given a legal research project or any other assignment, don't be afraid to ask questions about your assignment. Make sure you know what I need and my expectations of the assignment.

2.   The value of a legal internship or an internship in any other field is the exposure you get to this career. You might discover that you love what you will be doing, on the other hand it might be a clear message that this is not the field for you.

Sports Electronic Media Promotions Internship

Goals:

- Complete an internship for credit in a major radio or television sports environment to gain experience in communications, writing and strategy development and to understand the daily operations of the environment

- Complete credits requirement for degree major

- Use the internship to secure a position in the public relations industry

Mike attended the University of Florida as an electronic media major. He desired to take his internship in a major radio-broadcasting environment. Through friends and his university, he sourced multiple options, eventually landing an opportunity in a large broadcasting system, working in the promotions department with two other interns. To secure the internship he completed two interviews.

There were several factors that differentiated Mike from other candidates. First, Mike had successfully completed two previous internships while in high school, both in television environments. Second, he also worked a part-time job in a clothing retail store. Interviewers with the radio broadcasting system noted that Mike differentiated himself in how he dressed and presented himself, "I learned from working in retail how to dress for success. I realized that presenting myself with a crisp, professional appearance would make me standout compared to others." Mike's point was not that it took expensive clothes but more importantly, it was a professional appearance that said he "took the time to understand what the professional world expected of me. So, I always made sure my suit was clean and pressed, my shirts ironed and a tie that complimented my suit. They may not remember what I wore, but I wanted them to have an image of me as a professional."

In describing the value of his internship, he said while he learned a great deal, "I felt at times the work did not always challenge me. In hindsight I needed to be sure that the work I was assigned was a good match for my needs and expectations. An intern can't always control the situation, but you also have to learn to work closely with your employer to get assignments that match your skill level and challenge you."

Mike is now working in a communications firm with plans to enroll soon in the Georgetown University Sports Management MBA program. He hopes that a future internship supporting his MBA would be focused in a professional sports team environment.

Case Study: Change of Career Internship

Goals:

- Find a rewarding internship that builds upon previous work experience

- Maintain a somewhat flexible schedule that allows for a career search while still exploring opportunities with the present company

Drew is an MBA graduate from the University of Miami in Coral Gables, FL. Through the mentor program at his school, he was able to obtain an internship at Tech Products in the burgeoning Design District to supply high quality kitchen and bath cabinets. In addition to this internship, he wanted to get experience in the pharmaceutical industry and secured a simultaneous internship at IVAX Pharmaceuticals advising the VP of Business Development on new generic pharmaceutical product launches. This role allowed him to analyze how IVAX could capitalize on pending patent expirations of branded pharmaceuticals. Through this opportunity, Drew gained valuable hands-on experience as a competitively paid full-time intern. At the conclusion of this summer internship, he was asked to work part-time for the company to help turn around a struggling division. While still pursuing his MBA, he gladly accepted this part-time job assisting the Financial Customer Service Division in turning the department around and clearing up a backlog of pending requests for reimbursement. While complementing and building on the team atmosphere within the branded pharmaceutical division of IVAX, he was able to help lead a turnaround of the division, streamline operations, and improve response times for reimbursement from 6 months down to same day processing. Impressed with his diligence and ability to take initiative on difficult tasks, the president of the division invited Drew to lunch and discussed future opportunities with the company. Excited about these future opportunities, Drew began to collaborate with other divisions and became a go-to person for special projects. Unfortunately, IVAX was sold to a foreign company, and many of the employees were forced to seek alternative employment at other companies. Drew sought the advice of his mentor at Tech Products, and he decided to go to China to gain valuable international experience.

Drew was able to secure employment with Sias University, which was a pioneer in US educational partnerships in conjunction with Fort Hays State University. He began as a professor of Finance and Business Management, and was quickly promoted to oversee the Bachelor of General Studies Program and a team of 25 educational professionals in China. Involved in all aspects of the educational partnership between Sias and Fort Hays State, Drew was able to build on international exposure he gained in Miami, and apply it to this complex international environment – one that was predicated on developing relationships to implement change and strive for process improvement. After three years of steady process improvement, Drew decided to return to the US to capitalize on the incredible experience in China and utilize his knowledge and skills at a company in the US eager to improve and expand business operations in China.

Drew quickly found that the market downturn was dramatically affecting job prospects, and more companies were slowing in their hiring practices and promoting from within the company. Having returned to Miami, where he attended graduate school, he formulated a plan to capitalize on his international experience and help him network within circles that would be crucial in obtaining full time employment. He approached the Executive Director of the local Florida China Association and offered to provide them with critical analysis and customer outreach initiatives to demonstrate the value of the organization, and how it could provide value in the increasing trade partnerships between Florida and China. In addition, he developed a quarterly newsletter to apprise members on current events and new trends that could affect their goal of doing business in China, thus positioning the Association as one that has relevant expertise and knowledge when it comes to operations in China, a specialized field that was often new to the companies and their respective members.

One company in particular, Marcus & Millichap, was so impressed with Drew's ability and perseverance; they requested that he meet with an international client seeking to complete a real estate deal in Miami. The client was from Hong Kong and appreciated the opportunity to speak with a professional of similar background and understanding about his priorities in conducting the purchase of real estate in the US by international buyers. The senior associate was impressed with the interaction between Drew and his client, and offered Drew an internship to consult on real estate transactions with China and further hone his international experience and allow him to further develop an international network with business professionals.

Drew saw these internships as a practical demonstration of his abilities and the value he could add to the international operations of a company. He knew that with the rapidly changing landscape of international business, it was critical he stay sharp and evolve with the changing market dynamics in order to be able to step right in to a full time position for a company. The internships also provided him an opportunity to speak with potential emploeyers about specific examples of his applied leadership and business skills. Drew's goal was a full time job, but the internships proved to be a transitional gateway to make it back into the workforce. When asked what advice he would give to other students looking to gain valuable internship experience,

Drew offered several key points:

- Utilize professional and academic networks to develop the kind of relationships that can aid professional development and facilitate connections with decision makers within a company

- Focus on strong companies that have a history of employee development and promoting from within the organization. Internships with companies such as these, can provide critical opportunities to get a foot in the door and feel comfortable that once you do get your foot in the door, you will be given priority for positions and opportunities to advance within the company.

- Craft your own opportunity by identifying a need within a company, present yourself as a solution to that need and how you have the unique ability to implement your skills within the company. Because companies are more receptive to ideas that can improve operations while limiting investment exposure, interning with them first can be a win-win situation - the company receives your expertise in an area that may be unfamiliar to them, and the intern can demonstrate their competency in a manner that makes them an appealing candidate should a full time position become available. The company already knows the intern when he or she becomes a job candidate, therefore making him or her a more appealing candidate because much of the uncertainty that is an inherent risk with unfamiliar job candidates is alleviated.

- Seek out a mentor relationship with someone at the company that can oversee your progress and help maximize the potential benefits for the company from the internship. But bear in mind, it will probably be an informal mentorship.

- Use the internship as an opportunity to demonstrate your competency and diligence on a daily basis to prove that you are a fit for the corporate culture and can add value to the organization.

Public Relations and Communications Internship

Goals:

- Complete an internship for credit in a public relations firm to gain experience in communications, writing and strategy development and to understand the daily operations of a PR firm.

- Complete credit requirement for degree major

- Use the internship to secure a position in the public relations industry

Kaye Communications is an integrated *"seriously strategic"* marketing and public relations firm headquartered in Boca Raton, Florida, with a wide variety of clients including individuals, government, destination and hospitality, retail and corporate clients and associations. While the firm does not formally announce internships, it does have a practice of hiring two or three interns throughout the year. Bonnie Kaye, President and Chief Strategist of the firm is a champion of the internship process, "We've been welcoming interns for years and really value the process and the contribution these young minds provide. As much as we teach and coach them through "real life" agency work, we also learn and find new ideas and concepts from this new generation of students. I have appreciated the experience that our 2 sons have gained from their internships as well."

One of the great success stories for Kaye Communications is a recent intern, now a full-time employee. Mike graduated from the University of Florida with a major in Public Relations. His first goal upon graduation was to find a position as a public relations professional. To complete his degree requirements, Mike was required to complete a 3-month internship for credit. He desired to find an internship in the geographic area of his hometown in South Florida. His strategy was to search the Internet for public relations firms in the area. Second, he planned his internship as the final step in an academic requirement. His plan was that if successful in finding an internship, solid performance might result in being hired by the firm since he would not have to return to school for more classes.

He found Kaye Communications during his search and decided to call the firm to express his interest. Mike was like many students who are nervous making cold calls. Mike chuckled to himself "I was nervous to make that first call, so I decided to call the agency on Sunday and leave a message." On Monday he decided that he would call again, "By the time I made my second call, I was ready with my elevator speech." He said, "Hello my name is Mike and I left a message for you this weekend. I'm a University of Florida student, graduating this summer and I'm looking for an internship. I have been a great student and I'm very detail oriented. I'd love to discuss the possibilities of an internship with you." Mike was surprised to discover the person on the other end of the line was Bonnie Kaye, President of Kaye Communications. After a short conversation, Bonnie told Mike to send her his resume immediately. Mike was hired as an intern in the summer 2011.

According to President Bonnie Kaye, "Our goal is to find interns who are self-starters who take initiative to contribute to the firm and create a career in public relations." Our second goal is to find the right students and if they perform well, we hope the internship will turn into a permanent position as it has on three occasions." Bonnie was impressed with Mike's initiative and smiles at the fact of him calling the office on Sunday, "I'm glad Mike called again on Monday, He didn't realize that I'm also a (Florida) Gator, as well as our son, so of course I would be interested in a University of Florida grad."

Mike's role was to develop social media copy for various social media sites of clients and for the PR firms own social media site. The intern was also responsible for media research, telephone communications and message follow-up. After several weeks, Mike's role evolved, "My initial assignments were pretty basic but after a few weeks as I learned the ins and outs of agency work, Bonnie increased my responsibilities to include news releases, event planning, PowerPoint presentation assistance, and more. I was nervous, but I gained a lot of confidence each day." What Mike really enjoyed about his internship was that Kaye Communications is a small, but well known, family-owned firm, "I really felt that in this firm I would get more exposure to the real way a public relations firm operates. I was working directly with the President and was able to sit in and contribute to internal creative sessions and discussions with their top clients."

Mike's strategy worked. After the summer internship was completed and his final reports for his professors were turned in, a job opened when a full-time employee left the company, "The timing was perfect for me. I think Bonnie liked my work and was already interested in hiring me when an opening was available, but the departure of another person worked out perfectly. I love this job." Bonnie has appreciated how Mike has grown into position, "You never know how an intern will develop. This is a tough highly demanding business and my expectations are high. We give our interns the opportunity to 'apprentice', providing great experience and a good portfolio. Most do well, but we vet them well prior to joining us. They are assigned projects, some from start to finish, not merely given tasks. The self-starting, inquisitive and tenacious achievers do well here. I have written many reference letters for graduate school and entry positions and those that exceed expectations get glowing kudos."

"I look for interns that have had a good amount of core courses in the PR and marketing majors; third year students are ideal. I insist on good writing capabilities, ability to find the news or create it responsibly. Mike had that coming in... and this served him well."

Mike offered several pieces of advice to students looking for internships:

- Establish your goals for your internship and structure your search around those goals

- Internships in smaller firms give you an opportunity to put your name on the work you do, the stakes are high, but the work is going to be more challenging and rewarding

- Don't use the internship label to limit what you can do, this is a learning opportunity and you learn by stretching yourself

Case Study: Marketing

Goals:

- Gain real-life marketing work experience, including ability to use Spanish language skills

- Secure a paid internship that provides an opportunity to support her education

JJR is sophomore marketing major at Roosevelt University's online program in Chicago. While she has attended some classroom-based courses, the majority of her studies have been online. JJR is working her way through school with a good paying server job at a local high-end restaurant in downtown Chicago. She has 5 years of experience working in the restaurant service industry. JJR also has studied Spanish 4 years, is conversational in the language and has traveled to Spanish speaking environments.

JJR desired to gain experience in her field of study, however with her need to make money it would be difficult managing this goal. JJR decided to create an internship proposal for a new Latin restaurant which opened in downtown Chicago. She presented a proposal that combined her wait service experience, Latin culture exposure and Spanish language skills. Her idea was to do wait staff work but also do an internship by assisting the manager in developing a marketing strategy that attracted tourists to the restaurant. Her proposal suggested an approach to local downtown hotel concierges. She established goals and a plan on which hotels to approach, maps and other fun tools designed to attract customers. JJR also proposed that she be paid as normal for her restaurant duties but for her internship, she asked the manager to consider paying her $10 for each customer that submitted a referral card at the time they were presented a bill. The manager agreed to the entire structure except for the $10 referral fee. Instead, he agreed to $5 for each referral since he was also giving the customers $5 off each main course for accepting the referral and coming to the restaurant.

Sports Management Internship

Goals:

- Complete a requirement to complete MSPE

- Gain marketable experience for a sports management career

Marty completed an undergraduate degree in business marketing at the University of Notre Dame. His goal was to pursue a career in his passion of sports management.

While a senior in college, he sent out resumes to his local teams and was able to obtain seasonal work in the sales department of the Chicago White Sox. While with the Sox he discussed career paths with senior executives he wanted to emulate and he was advised to pursue a graduate degree.

During the application process for a Masters degree, he was able to leverage his experience with the White Sox into a Graduate Assistant role with Western Illinois University while pursuing his Masters of Science in Physical Education, with a concentration in Sports Management.

After completing his core classes and thesis, his final requirement was to complete an internship in the sports field. With the knowledge gained through his Master's degree, Marty had a better understanding of what specialization he wanted to concentrate on. He focused on major sports organizations in the marketing field and sent out hundreds of resumes in hopes of an internship offer.

After numerous interviews, Marty was able to obtain an internship with the Seattle SuperSonics in the Game Operations department. Although his Masters requirement was only a six week internship, Marty committed to his hiring manager to remain for the duration of the NBA season (8 months).

After just two weeks into the internship, some organizational restructuring created an open position in the Game Operations Department. Those two weeks had allowed Marty to gain the trust of his Directors and he was offered an entry-level position with the SuperSonics. So while he was completing his degree, he was being paid as a full-time member of the staff. Marty remained with the Super-Sonics for two seasons before moving on to the Boston Celtics as the Director of Marketing.

When asked what advice he would give other students looking to gain valuable internship experience, Marty offered 3 key points:

1.   While you're an undergraduate, build your resume by obtaining experience in the field you're pursuing, whether paid or voluntary. Give yourself an edge.

2.   When searching for an internship, cast a wide net. Don't limit yourself to your ideal organizations.

3.   Seek out guidance from individuals who are actually in the roles you hope to be in the future. You'll find that most successful businessmen enjoy telling their stories and giving advice.

Search Engine Optimization (SEO) Company Internship

Goals:

• Complete an internship to gain experience working in digital media

The SEO Group of Chicago is a boutique digital marketing firm that helps companies and their clients increase sales by offering tools, knowledge and experience to increase website traffic, conversions and sales. The company is known for its trademarked SEO audit tool that allows users to monitor and analyze Google rankings of their website and that of competitors. The CEO of the firm regularly hires one or two interns each year to work on various projects. SEO Group does not advertise for internships but instead uses networking and social media to find candidates. The firm desires individuals with excellent analytical skills and those that desire an environment where being a self-starter and an independent worker is rewarded.

Sarah was completing her sophomore year at the University of Illinois. She desired a 6-month internship to not only make some money but more important, she desired an environment where she could learn to interface with clients. During her search, she discovered the SEO Group through the company's Facebook Page. She posted a private note to the company resulting in the CEO responding to her note. While Sarah's internship was going to entail a great amount of "grunt" work, the CEO agreed to provide her client exposure, provided her primary work was on schedule. Sarah sat in on client meetings and gradually progressed to making small presentations to clients on various subjects. She received course credit and a small financial stipend at the end of her internship.

SEO Company Internship

Goals:

- Complete an internship to gain experience working in a journalism environment

RM was a freshman at the University of Notre Dame with intent to pursue a major in journalism. She had experience working in her high school newspaper and was a new reporter for the university newspaper. RM was unable to secure her desired internship for the summer, but found an opportunity working for a small social media-marketing firm. During the course of the summer she performed various tasks related to social media for clients including researching and writing client website blogs, posting to client Twitter and Facebook accounts and researching client social media opportunities.

Marketing Internship

Goals:

- Complete an internship to gain experience in developing and implementing a marketing strategy

Joan is a graduating marketing major from Florida Atlantic University. Her goal is to be a marketing professional in a marketing firm. She was not successful in securing an internship in a larger firm through the university career center. Joan approached several local not-for-profit organizations, looking for any internship work experience. She went online and sourced a list of not-for-profits through the local Chamber of Commerce and the United Way. Joan then made a list of agencies that would likely use marketing to advance their mission and proceeded to call these agencies. She put together five proposals for agencies who seemed to fit her needs. One agency offered an opportunity for the summer for the student to assist in the development of a marketing strategy to increase membership to the facilities publicly available fitness facility. After development of a targeted marketing strategy, the intern initiated a plan to begin recruiting members. This was not a paid internship, however with successful implementation of the program the facility gave a completion stipend of $2,000.

Journalism Internship

Goals:

- Complete an internship to gain experience in journalistic writing for newsprint organization

Sam is a junior journalism major from the University of Missouri, a well-known journalism school. He has experience writing for his high school newspaper and has been a sports writer for the Missouri campus newspaper. He desired an internship with a local newspaper that would enable him to go to summer school while working. While he was unable to secure a position writing for the local newspaper he was able to present a proposal to a St Louis-based online tourist magazine. Since Sam is from St Louis, he knows the area well and was able to secure an internship. The difficulty for Sam was that he was required to be in the St Louis office 2-days per week. This was an unpaid position but the company was willing to pay mileage for his trips home where he was able to stay with his parents, saving money.

Realty Firm Internship

Goals:

- Complete an international internship to gain specific experience within the field of international commercial real estate

Jerome is a graduate of Florida International University, Masters of International Real Estate online program. The program provides international real estate fundamentals and focuses on aspects of real estate that link domestic and international real estate transactions. While Jerome desires an international internship opportunity, he is not prepared to relocate internationally at this time due to a dual-career personal situation. Jerome lives in Washington, DC. His approach to securing an intern opportunity is focused in the local DC area where he began to search for agencies that work directly with foreign embassies to secure both residential and commercial real estate. He also cross-referenced his search with FIU graduates in the DC area that work in government or for foreign embassies. The search for real estate agencies working with embassies was not productive and therefore Jerome refocused on other Washington based real estate groups. He presented a proposal to a small agency suggesting the development of a marketing strategy to expand the agency to foreign embassy clients. This proposal included marketing research and Jerome directly approaching embassies to propose the new service.

Consumer Product Internship

Goals:

- Complete an internship to gain experience working in consumer product environment, beyond basic sales responsibilities

Megan is in her last year of her MBA program at NYU. She found her ideal internship online for the Disney Corporation in CA. However, summer relocation to CA was not an option. The job description of this internship was ideal.

- *This is an entry-level finance position when after spending a few years honing your financial and strategic skills in the real world, you're pursuing your MBA and looking for an exciting challenge for your summer break; Consider Disney Products for your MBA Summer Internship, where your work will help inspire memories that last a lifetime*

- *Our 10-12 week MBA intern program offers a unique opportunity to explore toys, fashion, food, stationery and more through finance and business development projects*

How You Can Contribute:

- *Collaborate with a team to complete a broad DC P-wide analysis incorporating data and processes from each line of business*

- *Work with finance teams to drive ongoing projects such as the annual operating plan, white space analyses, etc*

Impress Us With Your Smarts:

- *Ideally, you are a first-year student at a top-tier MBA School with 3-5 years of work experience prior to business school*

Encourage Us With Your Expertise:

- *Demonstrated analytical ability and strong communication skills*

- *Pre-MBA experience in consulting, consumer products, advertising, marketing and/or brand management preferred, with a minimum of 1-3 years of experience in financial analysis, planning and budgeting*

- *Deliverable-focused, strong work ethic and self-motivated*

- *Project orientation and ability to handle simultaneous functions*

- *Proven effectiveness working in a demanding, entrepreneurial environment*

- *Experience with market research and focus groups a plus, foreign language skills a plus.*

The description and skills required fit Megan's internship quite well. She modified this intern description into a proposal and submitted it to New York City-based zoos, museums and public parks. She was able to create the ideal summer internship at a local botanical garden assisting the director of the botanical garden store. For this internship, she received a summer-end stipend of $1,000. She had 2 projects during the summer: Megan completed a product inventory and updated the garden's online store.

Hotel Services Internship

Goals:

- Complete an internship to gain experience working in a consumer product environment, beyond basic sales responsibilities

Sally is seeking an internship in the hospitality industry. Her online search found a company offering a number of internships in this industry. The problem she quickly discovered was that the internships through this company require the intern to pay a fee. This is not unusual for certain industries where the demand is high. This company's internship program provides you with an opportunity to gain practical experience in a world-class hotel or resort in the USA. They match your hospitality, culinary or tourism management background with a variety of hospitality groups across the country, most of which are hotels.

Sally decided to conduct her own search into local hotels rather than large chain environments. This search resulted in finding a number of opportunities. However, in these smaller environments, Sally realized that the work, while rewarding in pay and experience also required her to clean hotel rooms and work in food service. At the end of the internship the experience gained was extensive and provided a broader set of skills than Sally had originally expected. Most important, she earned money needed to continue her education.

Sample 30 Second Elevator Speeches

The following are a series of sample elevator speeches to use in formulation of your speech. Remember, these speeches are designed to capture the attention and interest of perspective employers. They should demonstrate your confidence and ability to express concisely who you are, what you can do and what you want to do in 30-60 seconds.

Sample 30-Second Elevator Speech

Hi, my name is Jane Simons, and I am a senior Social Justice major at the University of Phoenix. I will graduate next year and I'm looking for an internship position that will allow me to use my communication and analytical skills. Over the past 2-years, I've been strengthening these skills through my work with a local community-based organization supporting voter registration efforts. Eventually, I'd like to develop social justice education programs to improve conditions for underprivileged in our community. My business law professor suggested I speak to you. Can you tell me how someone with my experience may fit into your organization?

Sample 30-Second Elevator Speech

It's a pleasure to meet you, I'm Adam Dison. I'm currently a senior at the University of Delaware and am studying Computer and Information Science. I hope to become a computer programmer when I graduate. I've had several internships where I worked on program application projects with a project team. I enjoy the creativity of this work, especially when it applies to developing business solutions. The position you have listed on Craig's List seems like it would be a perfect fit for someone with my skills.

Sample 30-Second Elevator Speech

It's a pleasure to meet you. I'm a senior, accounting major at the University of North Carolina and I'm looking for a summer internship in an accounting firm. I was fortunate to have completed a team practicum at a small firm last summer. One of the most important things I've learned in my academics and previous internship is the importance and need for integrity and trust in the accounting industry. Case studies I've followed regarding Enron and Worldcom highlight the changes and new habits and attitudes of the accounting function.

I anticipate finishing my academic work with 3.5 GPA while also participating in several extracurricular activities including writing for the campus online newspaper and working part time to support my tuition.

Sample 30-Second Elevator Speech

Hello, it's a pleasure to meet you. I'm in the first semester of an MBA program at Indiana University. I completed my undergrad degree in engineering at Purdue last May, and then spent my summers, practicing my French, traveling across France with friends. That was a great experience. But now I'm focused on completing my MBA in marketing. It's my plan to secure an internship this summer within a manufacturing environment where I can use my engineering skills and what I am learning in a marketing context to learn more about product development and marketing. I'm hoping to secure a paid position, but either way this internship is an important part of the curriculum. My father's partner, James Novell, suggested I speak with you. I found your background quite interesting. You seem to have a career similar to my goals.

Sample Internship Job Descriptions

The following are a series of sample internship job descriptions designed to assist you in developing your preferred internship opportunities. Job descriptions are quite diverse. There is no set way organizations design these documents. Your goal should be to design a job description in simple terms, insuring clarity of what you want to do and learn.

Sample Internship Proposal and Job Description

Dear Sir,

Position Title: Marketing Social Media Intern

Department: Marketing

Reports to: Manager of Social Media Development

Salary Range: Unpaid

Deadline: Must apply by Friday, June 22, 2012

Please include resume, cover letter and 3 references

POSITION SUMMARY

This position provides the opportunity to add valuable experience, notoriety and practical knowledge to your resume, growing your appeal with a broad range of employers. We provide the opportunity to learn more about the advertising and marketing business.

As an intern at Tech Multimedia, you would assist with a broad range of tasks including, but not limited to: managing client promotions and promotional fulfillment; attending client meetings and interaction with clients in a professional manner; relationship building and networking opportunities; updating and managing social media channels; attending and assisting with non-profit fundraising events which can include non-traditional hours and other duties as assigned.

This internship offers a unique opportunity to work in a boutique-advertising agency that is well respected in the industry. You will have exposure to various media outlets and marketing strategies that will be useful experience for career building. Additionally, upon successful completion of the internship, you can look forward to a recommendation from our organization.

HOURS

10-20 hours per week, M-F with some flexibility required and occasional hours during the evening/weekend depending on client events & needs. Internship duration will run August – December

JOB QUALIFICATIONS

- Must be highly organized, very detailed and an excellent communicator via email, phone and online chat

- Must be able to successfully and simultaneously manage many tasks of a broad variety in a timely and efficient manner

- Must be self-disciplined, able to work independently, proficient in time management and a self-starter looking to grow in the advertising industry

- Must have a positive attitude and a history of strong work ethic

- Must have a reliable car and driver's license

- Must have a home-based office, as well as a computer, printer, and Internet connection

- Must be able to work hard but keep it fun

JOB REQUIREMENTS

- *Education:* Must currently be enrolled in four-year college for marketing, public relations, communications or business. Applicants must be at the junior or senior level with at least a 3.0 GPA

- *Experience:* Samples of past work or examples of capabilities

- *Required skills:* Microsoft Word, Excel, Outlook and familiarity with social media outlets such as Facebook, Twitter and Pinterest

- *Preferred skills*: PowerPoint and familiarity with social media outlets such as YouTube and Flickr

Sample Internship Job Description

Finance or Accounting Internship

Description

Company is looking for a Finance/Accounting intern. The student filling this position will handle a wide range of important duties.

Responsibilities

- Assist with month-end financial reports
- Post journal entries
- Help with accounts receivable, payable and bank statement reconciliation
- Assist with audits
- Balance sheet reconciliation
- Work with the finance team on yearly forecasting efforts
- Manage the monthly tracking of our physical inventory
- Support the payment processing team
- Data entry
- Credit checks

Requirements

Applicants should be Business, Finance, Economics or Accounting majors with proficiency in Microsoft Office applications. Attention to detail, the ability to multi-task and excellent communication skills are all essential to this position.

Majors

Business, Finance, Economics, Accounting

Sample Internship Job Description

General Duties/Description:

One of two professional staff, twelve-month contract Admissions Counselor Intern positions. Full-time.

Responsibilities include: Counseling prospective freshman and transfer applicants; responding to admissions inquiries via phone and email; representing the University at on-campus information sessions; giving campus tours on back-up basis; covering reception desk on back-up basis; traveling throughout Washington to represent the University at college fairs; reviewing freshman and transfer applications; assisting in outreach and recruitment programs; and other duties as assigned. We are looking for someone who will be a new or recent University graduate, is enthusiastic about the University, has a strong work-ethic, exercises sound judgment, and is skilled at public speaking and writing. This would be an ideal job for someone who would like to work for one year before going to graduate school.

When you apply, in addition to your resume, please include a brief cover letter describing your interest in this position.

Requirements: Bachelor's degree from the University by the start of employment. Must have the energy and drive to work in a fast-paced office. Involvement in University clubs or organizations. During fall and spring recruitment seasons, this position requires the ability to work odd hours and some weekends; travel to remote locations; load and transport admissions materials, displays and other equipment. Strong interpersonal and writing skills are necessary, including public speaking skills and the ability to present the University in a positive way to diverse populations. Candidates need not have completed their bachelor's degree at the time they apply; however, they must complete their degree by their start date. Must be able to start no later than August 1.

Desirable: The ability to start mid to late June is preferred. The ideal candidate would be a recent graduate (by the start of employment) and preferably have already represented the University in some capacity (for example, as a Student Ambassador, Tour Guide, RA, Orientation Leader). As a role model for prospective students, the candidate should have a strong and positive University experience as both a student and campus community member.

Financial Analyst Internship

Goals:

- Complete an internship to gain experience working in Financial Services firm.

This is an entry-level finance position for a summer internship. You will be involved in many areas of corporate finance support in a fast paced technology company, and experience many different services of the finance function. You will most likely be asked to perform increasingly responsible work over the first year as we develop your basic understanding and a foundation for future growth and responsibility.

Job Requirements:

- Excellent written and verbal skills; excellent listener

- Demonstrated successful academic, social and extracurricular record

- Must have a sense of humor

- "Work Hard, Play Hard" mentality a must

- Strong teamwork required; demonstrated success is a requirement

- Desire to work in a fast-paced, dynamic environment with competing priorities

- Strong skills in spreadsheets, systems and processes

- Curious personality with a desire to understand "how things work" and "how things are related"

Education and Experience:

- B.S Degree in Finance or Accounting or equivalent

- 0-2 years of financial planning and analysis experience in a large growth company

- Demonstrated ability to meet deadlines and produce accurate results

Sample Internship Job Description

Marketing Communications Internship

Functional Area(s): Marketing Communications

Department: Come join GCOM, General Mills' Marketing Communications division. GCOM is a centralized organization that provides integrated marketing services, including promotion support, digital support, public relations, multi-cultural, social media and more! As an intern in GCOM, you will work with one of our Integrated Marketing Communication teams and spend 12 weeks at our Corporate Headquarters learning from our internal functional teams. While the assignments and projects vary depending on the business needs, we provide you with meaningful marketing communications assignments that will have a real impact on our business. Not only will you receive exposure to the consumer products industry, you'll learn how to build effective marketing campaigns and stronger brand equities

Job Description: As a Marketing Communication Intern, you will work closely with your Manager and Business Teams to develop integrated marketing programs consistent with overall brand marketing objectives.

You will be challenged to recognize opportunities and generate new ideas that have a positive impact on the business. You will assist in coordinating, developing and executing integrated marketing program communications and materials. You will also be responsible for reporting program status and final results to your assigned brands through individual and group updates and presentations.

By acting as a key liaison between Marketing, Sales, internal and external partners and agencies, you'll develop a broad network of effective working relationships with agencies, vendors, tie-in partners, customers and colleagues. You will also get a chance to meet and collaborate with other integrated marketing communications interns from different schools and locations.

Key Competencies for Position

- **Strategic Thinking with External Focus:** Understands business issues and implications of decisions on performance

- **Creativity:** Demonstrates the ability to bring fresh thinking to problems/opportunities and to generate innovative courses of action to meet business needs

- **Initiative with Bias for Results:** Displays proactive urgency, focused on specific, ambitious goals combined with personal accountability for achieving results

- **Business Knowledge:** Demonstrates broad business knowledge and understands key business drivers

- **Relationship Building:** Effectively builds fair and mutually beneficial relationships with other employees, outside agencies, vendors and business partners

Expectations of Candidates

- Ability to collaborate and work in a team environment

- Outstanding organizational skills

- Ability to manage projects while meeting deadlines

- Superior interpersonal and communications skills

Location: General Mills World Headquarters, Minneapolis,

Preferred Education

- MS or MBA Degrees Preferred

- B.S. or B.A. degree in Business, Marketing, Advertising, Journalism, Communications or Public Relations

Sample Letters of Introduction

In this section you have been provided sample formats and actual Letters of Introduction. These letters are of great importance and should be concise and well written to gain the attention of prospective employers.

Sample Letter Of Introduction Format

First Name Last Name

2930 Tuscany Way

Chicago, IL 60657

Today's Date

Contact Name

Business Name

Address

City, PA zip code

Dear_____:

1st paragraph

- Explain how you know about this company/classroom

- Explain any connections you have to this company/classroom or explain what you know about the company/classroom that makes you enthusiastic

- Explain your understanding of what you will be doing there

2nd paragraph

- Explain what your skills are that will help them

- Point out items from your resume that are of interest to the internship supervisor

- Explain how you will act during the internship

3rd paragraph

- Thank the internship supervisor for their time

- Let them know that you look forward to interning in their company or classroom

- Explain dates of internship and make sure you provide reliable contact information including your phone numbers and email address

Sincerely,

Your name

Phone #

Email

Sample Letter Of Introduction

Dear Mr./Ms. Last Name:

I am interested in a finance internship and I would like to inquire about an opportunity with ABC Company. ABC's Professional Leadership Program has been recommended to me as one of the most highly regarded corporate finance internship programs in the industry. I would be interested in learning more about the company and about available internship opportunities.

I will complete my Bachelor's Degree in Accounting from Capella University. In addition, I completed two internships focusing on finance and spent a summer working for Financial Accounts Corporation at its' New York City headquarters.

My resume, which is enclosed, contains additional information on my experience and skills. I would appreciate the opportunity to discuss the leadership program with you and to provide further information on my candidacy. I can be reached via my cell phone, 123-456-7890 or by email at bbbb@gmail.com.

Thank you for your time and consideration. I look forward to speaking with you about this exciting opportunity.

Sincerely,

Name

Email

Sample Letter Of Introduction

Dear Mr. or Ms. Last Name:

I am writing to express my interest in an internship position this summer. I am currently a first year Business Management student studying at Bowling Green University. For the past year, I have developed extensive experience and knowledge from my program and would like to apply these experiences and knowledge for this internship.

From my research on MNN Corporation, I feel that your company would offer me an outstanding opportunity to expand my skills and learn more about business management. I believe this firm is the right place to challenge myself through critical thinking, creativity and innovativeness. This internship is beneficial to me at this stage of my development process because it fits my educational background, my continuing willingness to learn new things and represents a perfect chance to improve my skills. Furthermore, I am a quick learner, hard-working, ambitious person, motivated by goal achievements, having a multi-perspective approach towards a situation. Nothing provides me with more satisfaction than bringing a contribution to the success of a project.

The accompanying resume can provide you with greater details of my background and what I have to offer.

Thank you for your time and consideration.

Sincerely yours,

First Name Last Name

312-555-5555

jane@janedoe.com

Sample Letter Of Introduction

Date

Name

Address

Mobile Phone

Email Address

LinkedIn URL

Regarding: Internship Proposal

Dear Ms. Last Name:

I am interested in applying for a scientific research summer internship position.

I have had a great deal of laboratory experience in chemistry, biology, and geology, both indoors and in the field. In the lab, I have performed chemical reactions and I am currently using microscopes to observe many specimens. In environmental field studies, I have conducted outdoor labs to assess water chemistry.

Last summer, I worked as conservation assistant at Clumber National Park. I am seeking to complement this outdoor experience with a research internship in order to acquire the background necessary for a future career in scientific research.

Attached please find my proposal for this internship, which includes:

- My resume

- A proposed job description detailing my ideal internship which can be adjusted to meet your needs and expectations

- A proposed Performance Evaluation Format that outlines how my performance may be monitored and feedback documented

I believe that I would be an asset to your program. This internship would provide me with the ideal opportunity to contribute to the success of your organization and to expand my research and my professional knowledge, skills and abilities.

I will call next week to see if you agree that my qualifications meet your needs and expectations. If so, I hope to schedule an interview at a mutually convenient time. I look forward to speaking with you.

Thank you for your consideration.

Sincerely,

Signature

First and Last Name

Sample Letter Of Introduction

Dear Mr. James:

As a junior chemical engineering major at the University of New Excellence, I was pleased to find your profile in the New Excellence Career Advisory Network (NECAN). I am currently exploring careers in the pharmaceutical industry and would greatly appreciate a chance to speak with you regarding internship opportunities and to learn more about "Big Pharma" companies and the industry in general.

Although my primary motivation is to obtain an internship or preferably a permanent position, your insights and advice are valuable to me. I would welcome any assistance you might be able to offer regarding the fields of engineering or research.

The NECAN system unfortunately does not allow attachments, but upon receiving your email reply I would be happy to send you a copy of my resume and a proposal for the type of position I am seeking. I realize that you are very busy, but I hope we can schedule a time to speak by phone in the near future. I look forward to your reply. Thank you in advance!

Sincerely,

Jan Smythe

UR Chemical

Engineering Class of 2012

jsmith@une.edu

222.333.4444

Sample Letter Of Introduction

Dr. Ms. Travers:

After researching your company in social media sites, I am contacting you to ask for assistance with my search for a 6 month internship within the Commercial Real Estate industry. As a senior at the University of Maryland, it would be very helpful if I could speak or meet with a "career role model" and I respectfully request any consideration, referrals, or advice you might offer.

If you respond to this query and share your email address, I will provide you a copy of my resume. When you review my resume I hope you determine my academic and experiential background - including project management, business acumen and written communications - worthy of your time and agree to conduct a phone or in person information conversation.

After we do speak or meet, I also hope you would find me a strong enough candidate to consider me for an internship opportunity. If no opportunities exist within your area, perhaps you would refer me to colleagues at your firm or other firms in in the greater Baltimore area. Most important, while your consideration would be ideal, any advice or counsel regarding how to progress down a career path similar to yours would be much appreciated.

Sincerely,

James McDonald

Sample Letter Of Introduction

Dear Mr. Bocadelray:

After learning that you, a University of Wisconsin alumnus, are practicing environmental law I was inspired to email you. I will also become a U of W alum in June of this year and I would very much appreciate a few minutes of your time by phone so I could ask a few questions about your career biography and seek your advice and counsel. At this stage, as a senior, I am curious regarding issues related to when to apply to law school, the advantages or disadvantages of first seeking paralegal positions, and how to focus my studies on environmental issues.

Attached is a copy of my resume to quickly share information regarding my academic background. I also attached my thoughts regarding an internship for this summer that would hopefully provide me greater insight into the field. If it is more convenient to continue to correspond by email and you would like me to provide four or five specific questions, please let me know. While an email response to this request would be welcomed, because you must be so very busy, I will call soon to discuss your reactions to my request for an information conversation. Thank you.

Jennifer Brown

Email

2011 Political Science and Anthropology Dual Major

Sample Letter Of Introduction

Dear Ms. Jacobson:

Greetings from The Ohio State University! I am a graduating senior studying Biomedical Engineering at OSU. Working with the Career and Alumni Centers here on campus, I was able to identify you as a potentially helpful networking contact. Specifically, I am seeking the guidance and support of alumni in the medical device field as I search for a full-time position or post-baccalaureate internship in quality assurance and testing. I have applied online for an entry level QA position at your firm and would appreciate any referrals you might be able to make to Human Resources or a hiring manager, so that I might follow up appropriately.

You will see from my attached resume that my background includes research in several areas as well as a senior design project in which I built and tested a prototype of a testing system with a team of fellow BME students. I believe I am thus well qualified for this position and hope you feel confident in making such a referral.

Additionally, I would welcome an opportunity to meet with you at your convenience in order to gain your insights and advice regarding my search.

Thank you in advance and I look forward to your reply. Go Buckeyes!

Sincerely,

Joe Ireland

Biomedical Engineering

Class of 2011

jlreland@OSU.edu

333.444.5555

Sample Letter Of Introduction

Dear Mr. Green:

I was excited to learn that you graduated from the University of Pittsburgh the same year as my father, Don Brown. I am currently a junior at Pitt and looking forward to a law career. It is my understanding that you practice tort law with Smith, Smith and Smith. I hope you will answer a few questions about your career biography and offer some advice and counsel. As a junior, I am curious regarding issues related to when to apply to law school, the advantages or disadvantages of first seeking paralegal positions, and, honestly, I am actively seeking internship or shadowing opportunities for the spring semester and summer of 2014.

While I sincerely wish to learn more about your career and educational biography, any consideration for internships or shadowing opportunities at your firm would be appreciated. Referrals to colleagues at your firm, or at other Philadelphia area firms, ideally in tort law, would also be much appreciated. The attached resume provides information regarding my academic and practical experiences. Through a brief telephone conversation, I can gain your insights and, after, I hope you would feel confident supporting my internship search efforts. If it is more convenient to correspond by email, I can provide four or five specific questions, and we can progress appropriately. A response to this request would be most welcomed. Thank you in advance for your time.

Jennifer Brown '11

Political Science and Anthropology Dual Major

email

Sample Linkedin Letters Of Introduction

Introducing yourself on LinkedIn is different than a regular letter of introduction. LinkedIn has rules and these rules are designed to insure people are not bombarded with requests to link for solicitation purposes. However, alumni from your school and those persons in groups you have joined will generally be open to linking with you.

Sample LinkedIn Letter Of Introduction

Dear Mr. Unique:

As a sophomore contemplating majors in communication and broadcast journalism, I was very excited to see your entry in the Career Advisory Network/Linked In Group. I sincerely hope you will agree to speak with me by phone, meet in person, or answer a few questions via email.

Basically, I want to conduct a brief information conversation in order to learn more about your career biography and to seek advise on internship ideas. I believe the more I learn about how alumni have applied their undergraduate UM experiences to successful careers within my field, the more academic and career direction I will have. And, during our conversation, I hope to gain your insights, advice and, ideally, consideration for a summer internship, shadowing or volunteer experiences as well.

Because I do not have direct access to your email, and would like to share my background via a resume, your response to this request to my email address, Johson@um.edu, would be most enthusiastically appreciated.

Sample Linkedin Letter Of Introduction

Dear Mr. Russell:

As a May graduate of the University of Notre Dame, I look forward to connecting with you and other ND alum as I start my career.

My degree was in business finance and I hope to network with you as I continue my search for an internship in the financial services industry. My Notre Dame experience has been wonderful and of course like all of us I was excited about our football team's success. I look forward to connecting with you.

Thank you for your time and Go Irish!

Donald Sims

Email

Sample Follow-Up And Thank You Letters

Follow up and thank you letters keep your interest and face alive in the minds of prospective employers. Like Letters of Introductions, it's important to be concise and leave the employer with a positive impression of their interactions with you.

Sample Follow-Up And Thank You Letter

Dr. Ms. Travers:

Thank you for your time and my interview yesterday for your marketing internship. I was very impressed with ABC Company and the staff I met. I learned a great deal that confirmed my interest in your company and desire to complete an internship within your marketing department. Especially interesting and exciting to me was the opportunity to work on marketing communications projects within your social media environment.

I would like to confirm my understanding that second interviews will be conducted within the next 2 weeks. My course schedule permits me to be available any afternoon Monday, Wednesday and Fridays and all day Thursday. Per your request, I attached a copy of my last market strategy project. I believe you will find it interesting.

In conclusion, I believe my strong written and verbal communication skills and my nature to be a self-starter will be seen as valuable assets to you and the team. Again, thank you for your time. I look forward to hearing from you.

Sincerely

Signature

First Name Last Name

Phone number

Email

Sample Follow-Up And Thank You Letter

Dear Mr. Donaldson:

I sincerely appreciate the time you took today interviewing me for the position of Social Service Intern. After learning more about Daycare Corporation and its goals, the possibility of joining the company is even more exciting.

The information you provided has further convinced me that I can make a positive contribution towards the care and support of children served by your company. The position we discussed is well suited to my strengths and skills and my previous 5-years of experience providing babysitting services is an excellent match with the job requirements.

I am looking forward to hearing from you. If you require any additional information, please feel free to call.

Thank you for your time and consideration.

Sincerely

Signature

First Name Last Name

Phone number

Email

Sample Follow-Up And Thank You Letter

Dear Mr. Cummings:

I would like to take this opportunity to thank you for the interview this morning. I was keenly motivated by the details you provided on the Realty.com internship. I would like to confirm my strong interest in this entry-level position.

Your clear explanation of the requirements of the job reinforced my confidence that my education and background are a good match for this position and that I would prove to be an asset to the company. I have always been considered an engaged, diligent worker and I would cherish the opportunity to demonstrate my commitment and ability to excel in this job.

Again, thank you for the time. I look forward to hearing from you soon.

Sincerely

Signature

First Name Last Name

Phone number

Email

Sample Resumes

There are many formats and opinions on how to develop an effective resume. These samples provide you a number of options. Most important is to be clear, accurate and avoid typos and grammar mistakes.

BAD Sample Resume

SALLY JAMES
123 Diversey Chicago, Il. 60657
(312) 325-3255
Sally.James@uofm.edu

Education
• Downtown High School Chicago, IL	June 2010
• University of Michigan B.S. Business Administration	Anticipated May 2014

Work Experience
University of Michigan Student Phone Center Ann Arbor, MI   Jan. 2011 - present
- Placed personalized phone calls to potential donors to solicit support for the University. Individually raised more than $30,000 in donations for Michigan's annual fund and other University organizations

The Gap, Ann Arbor, MI   2010
- Sales Clerk

The Jacobs Group, Chicago, Illinois   Summer 2010 - intern
- Wrote articles for client websites and blogs and did web research to assist associates with their current assignments

University of Michigan Organizations
- Wolverine Newspaper Reporter, 2010 - 2011
- University of Michigan Student Council
- Jazz Piano Company of University of Michigan

High School Honors
- AP Scholar with Honor - National Honor given to students based on scores on Advanced Placement Exams
- Commended Student for the National Merit Program - National Honor given to students with the top 2% of SAT scores in the United States
- Academic Scholar – Award Given to the top 25 students in each class graduating from Downtown High School

Service
- Tutoring program for underprivileged grade school students
- Volunteer: Chicago Home for the Aged
- Fundraising and support of Adolescents in Need Program
- Volunteer: Cure for Cancer 5K Run

References Available Upon Request

Compare this resume to a GOOD version of Sally's resume.

GOOD Sample Resume

Sally JAMES
123 Diversey Chicago, Il. 60657
(312) 325-3255
Sally.James@uofm.edu

University of Michigan Junior seeking a challenging internship that will enable me to put into use my professional and personal skills and formal education in support of broadening my professional experience and enhancing my career opportunities. My skills include:

* Academic Excellence
* Integrity
*Accountability

* Bilingual (7 years Spanish)
* Teamwork
* Global Travel - 15 countries

EDUCATION

University of Michigan	B.S. Business Administration (GPA: 3.4/4.0)	May 2014
Downtown High School	Advanced Placement (GPA: 3.9/4.40)	June 2010

WORK EXPERIENCE

University of Michigan
Student Phone Center   Jan. 2011 – present
* Responsible for alumni donor solicitation supporting the University's annual giving campaign.
* Raised in excess of $30,000 against a target goal of $20,000.

The Wolverine Newspaper   2010 – 2011
* Student reporter for University of Michigan newspaper

The Gap   2010
* Responsible for providing customer service and sales floor coverage

The Jacobs Group, Chicago, Illinois
Internship   Summer 2010
* Responsible for providing copywriting support for a Chicago based digital marketing firm
* Responsibilities included writing client articles, blogs and tweets, conducting market research and assisting associates with various marketing assignments.

COLLEGIATE EXTRACURRICULAR ACTIVITIES

• Reporter, Wolverine Student Newspaper	2010 - 2013
• Member, Student International Business Council	2010 - 2012
• Jazz Pianist, Jazz Company of Michigan	2011 - 2010

HIGH SCHOOL HONORS AND EXTRACURRICULAR ACTIVITIES

* National Advanced Placement Scholar with Honors
* National Merit Scholarship Program
* Academic Scholar –Top 25 Students of Downtown High School

- Reporter, Downtown High School
- Downtown High School Debate Team

COMMUNITY-BASED SERVICE

- Tutoring program for underprivileged grade school students
- Volunteer: Chicago Home for the Aged
- Fundraising and support of Adolescents in Need Program
- Volunteer: Cure for Cancer 5K Run
- Blood Donor
- Sunday School Teacher for K-3rd Grade

References Available Upon Request

Good Sample Resume

Kris Brooks
San Francisco, CA 11111
Brooks.K@abc.edu
555-555-5555

Education

Ohio State University, Columbus, OH   GPA 3.88/4.0   May 2013
- Candidate for Combined Bachelor/Master of Science in Chemical Engineering
- Honors/Awards: Provost Undergraduate Research Award, Dean's List, and Dean's Scholarship

  Activities: Ohio State University Chapters of Tau Beta Pi Honor Society (Vice President), American Institute of Chemical Engineers and International Society Pharmaceutical Engineers, Intramural Soccer

Skills

- Computer: MATLAB, C++, AutoCAD, Aspen Plus Simulator, Microsoft Office
- Analytical: HPLC, X-ray Diffraction, Gas Chromatography, Dynamic Light Scattering Particle Size

Professional Work Experience

Ohio State University, Columbus, OH   July 2012- Present

Advanced Drug Delivery Research Laboratory
- Undergraduate/Graduate Researcher
  - Recipient of Provost Undergraduate Research Award for work on retinal tissue engineering
  - Responsible for developing and testing natural matrix-based cell delivery vehicles to promote retinal regeneration

Ford Institute of Technology, Detroit, MI   January 2011-August 2011

Center for Continuous Manufacturing partnership with Novartis Corporation
- Pharmaceutical Manufacturing Research Development Co-op
  - Responsible for integrating and operating a continuous powder flow system in a large-scale pilot plant
  - Implemented equipment including a continuous dryer, gravimetric feeder, and vacuum conveyor to fulfill integration requirements of further downstream processes
  - Analyzed powder uniformity and characterization using HPLC, Gas Chromatography, and X-ray Diffraction methods
  - Provided support for downstream unit operations during final system test run in June 2012

Tectrabio, Inc., Cleveland, OH   January 2010-June 2010

Biopharmaceutical Company developing synthetic nanoparticle vaccines and immunotherapies
- Laboratory Technician Co-op
  - Completed bench-top chemistry experiments and aseptic small-scale production runs of various nanoparticle formulations

136

o Prepared chemicals, solutions, glassware, sterile workspace, and samples for formulation studies, biological studies, and nanoparticle manufacture

Additional Work Experience

Ohio State University, Columbus, OH   September 2011-September 2012

Department of Chemical Engineering

- Peer Tutor for Transport Processes and Thermodynamics Courses
- Work with underclassmen enrolled in Transport Processes and Thermodynamics
- Host review sessions and provide office hours to assist students with homework assignments as well as with test and quiz preparation

Good Sample Resume

Emily INTERNER
12405 Riverside Drive, Houston, TX 78248
210-555-1210 (home)
210-555-1955 (mobile)
ebrown@hilldaleinternet.net

Objective
Seeking an internship or full-time permanent position in the publishing industry where I can utilize my organizational, communication, and writing skills

WORK EXPERIENCE
Freelance Website Copywriter, *Houston, Texas*   *Jan. 2010 - present*
- Wrote and proofread copy for marketing materials promoting educational assessments

Writers For Hire, *Houston, Texas*   *May 2012 – Sept. 2012*
- Wrote ad copy for newsletters promoting nutritional supplement products for health store chain
- Conducted product research and wrote product descriptions for customers

INTERNSHIPS
Houston Statesman, *Houston, Texas*   *May 2012 – Sept. 2012*
Editorial Intern
- Worked with the Editorial Assistant and staff writers to research stories and edit text
- Assisted in producing the *Around The City* section in the *Houston Statesman*, which lists all the notable cultural events taking place in the city for the month
- Helped to generate story ideas at the monthly Editorial Board meetings and performed various editorial and research tasks that assisted in the production of the newspaper

Harcourt Assessment, Inc., *Houston, Texas*   *2011*
Marketing Intern
- Wrote and proofread copy for ads, catalogs and flyers promotional materials

SKILLS AND ABILITIES
Computer Skills
- Hardware: PC and Macintosh
- Software: Microsoft Office, Microsoft Word, Outlook, Quark, Windows, Excel, PowerPoint, Page Maker, Vegas Pro, Pro Acid, Sound Forge, Premier and various other media related software.

Other Skills:
- Video and Audio Production; Journalism Experience; Script Writing; Writing for the Media;
- Creative Writing; Aesthetics of Vision and Sound; Media Ethics; Public Relations; and Advertising

VOLUNTEER HISTORY
- Tannen Blood Center, Assistant Systems Clerk   2011
- American Red Cross, Relief volunteer   2010-211

EDUCATION
The University of Texas — Houston, TX   May 2012
Bachelor of Arts — Communications

Sample Resume

Elizabeth Jameson
6 Pine Street, Arlington, VA 12333
Home: 555.555.5555
Cell: 566.486.2222
Email: phjones@vacapp.com

EDUCATION

MLK Jr. High School, Atlanta, GA	2002 – 2006
Spellman College (Freshman) Anticipated Graduation	2010

EXPERIENCE

Pet Sitter: 2004 - Present
- Provides pet sitting services including dog walking, feeding and yard care

Child Care: 2002 - Present
- Provides child-care for several families after school, weekends and during school vacations

ACHIEVEMENTS
- National Honor Society: 2004, 2005 and 2006
- Academic Honor Roll: 2002 - 2006

Volunteer Experience
- Big Brother / Big Sisters
- Arlington Literacy Program
- Run for Life

Interests / Activities
- Member of Arlington High School Tennis Team
- Girl Scouts
- Piano

Computer Skills
- Proficient with Microsoft Word, Excel, PowerPoint and Internet

John Applicant
123 Main St. New York, New York 12345
John.Applicant@email.com

EDUCATION
ABC College, Sarasota Station, NY, May 2009
- Bachelor of Science Candidate
- Major: Anthropology

RELEVANT EXPERIENCE
Campus Representative- Uptown Computers, Sarasota Station, NY   02/2009 – Present
- Plan and execute numerous marketing campaigns per month
- Work with campus bookstore to drive sales of Apple products
- Host demo tables and educational workshops
  Act as a resource for existing and prospective Apple customers

Summer Marketing Intern, National Museum Society, New York, NY   05/2008 - 08/2008
- Assist with planning, installation and de-installation of exhibitions
- Develop bi-monthly news bulletin
- Design web pages publicizing events
- Create online slideshows of organizations events
- Prepare instruction manual for staff members on how to create online slideshows and basic template for web page
- Assist in all other administrative duties of the office

Resident Assistant, Jacobs Junior College, Sarasota Station, NY   09/2008 – Present
- Ensure safety and management of residential building
- Act as support network for incoming freshman and other residents
- Plan and execute community building programs
- RA of the Month Award (November 2008)
  RA of the Semester Award (December 2008)

Assistant, Career Services, ABC College, Sarasota Station, NY   09/2007 - Present
- Contacting alumni to update career information
- Updating internship database via phone and email
- Publicizing office events via Facebook
- Scheduling appointments and assisting students register and find information

ADDITIONAL EXPERIENCE
Website Developer, UJIMA, ABC College, Sarasota Station, NY   01/2007 - 05/2008
- Development and maintenance of club's website (publicize events via website)
- Plan club programs including guest speakers and dinners

Respect Matters Campaign, New York College, Sarasota Station, NY   01/2007 - 05/2008
- Develop campus-wide campaign promoting diversity efforts on campus
- Peer advisor to two leadership focused groups for incoming freshman and sophomore leaders
- Collaborate with other student groups to sponsor diversity-focused programs

Student Government Association, New York College, Sarasota Station, NY   01/2007 - 12/2007
- Elected by student body to serve as representative in student senate to oversee schools clubs, organizations and student led initiatives
- Interview and recommend candidates for Student Government positions

Technical Skills
Software - MS Office, Adobe Creative Suite: Photoshop, Dreamweaver, In Design and Flas

Sample - Student Intern Performance Evaluation

Please rate the intern's performance in the following areas:

Term of Internship: ___ Sum ___ Fall ___ Spring   Date of Evaluation: _____

Intern's Name: _____

Organization Name: _____

Supervisor Name: _____

Rating Scale: **1 = Excellent** - far exceeded expectations

2 = Good - met and exceeded expectations

3 = Satisfactory - met expectations, continues to develop

4 = Fair - somewhat met expectations, but needs improvement

5 = Unsatisfactory - did not meet expectations

	1	2	3	4	5
1) Oral communication	1	2	3	4	5
2) Written communication	1	2	3	4	5
3) Initiative	1	2	3	4	5
4) Interaction with staff	1	2	3	4	5
5) Attitude	1	2	3	4	5
6) Dependability	1	2	3	4	5
7) Ability to learn	1	2	3	4	5
8) Planning and organization	1	2	3	4	5
9) Professionalism	1	2	3	4	5
10) Creativity	1	2	3	4	5
11) Quality of work	1	2	3	4	5
12) Productivity	1	2	3	4	5
13) Appearance	1	2	3	4	5
14) Adaptability to organization's culture/policies	1	2	3	4	5
15) Integrity and Trust	1	2	3	4	5
16) Leadership Courage	1	2	3	4	5
17) OVERALL PERFORMANCE	1	2	3	4	5

Comments and impressions regarding the intern's performance against goals established:

Describe the intern's greatest improvement opportunity:

Describe the intern's greatest strength:

Department of Labor Wage and Hour Internship Rules and Regulations

Fact Sheet #71: Internship Programs Under The Fair Labor Standards Act

This fact sheet provides general information to help determine whether interns must be paid the minimum wage and overtime under the Fair Labor Standards Act for the services that they provide to "for-profit" private sector employers.

Background

The Fair Labor Standards Act (FLSA) defines the term "employ" very broadly as including to "suffer or permit to work." Covered and non-exempt individuals who are "suffered or permitted" to work must be compensated under the law for the services they perform for an employer. Internships in the "for-profit" private sector will most often be viewed as employment, unless the test described below relating to trainees is met. Interns in the "for-profit" private sector who qualify as employees rather than trainees typically must be paid at least the minimum wage and overtime compensation for hours worked over forty in a workweek.*

The Test For Unpaid Interns

There are some circumstances under which individuals who participate in "for-profit" private sector internships or training programs may do so without compensation. The Supreme Court has held that the term "suffer or permit to work" cannot be interpreted so as to make a person whose work serves only his or her own interest an employee of another who provides aid or instruction. This may apply to interns who receive training for their own educational benefit if the training meets certain criteria. The determination of whether an internship or training program meets this exclusion depends upon all of the facts and circumstances of each such program.

The following six criteria must be applied when making this determination:

1. The internship, even though it includes actual operation of the facilities of the employer, is similar to training which would be given in an educational environment;

2. The internship experience is for the benefit of the intern;

3. The intern does not displace regular employees, but works under close supervision of existing staff;

143

4. The employer that provides the training derives no immediate advantage from the activities of the intern; and on occasion its operations may actually be impeded;

5. The intern is not necessarily entitled to a job at the conclusion of the internship; and

6. The employer and the intern understand that the intern is not entitled to wages for the time spent in the internship.

If all of the factors listed above are met, an employment relationship does not exist under the FLSA, and the Act's minimum wage and overtime provisions do not apply to the intern. This exclusion from the definition of employment is necessarily quite narrow because the FLSA's definition of "employ" is very broad. Some of the most commonly discussed factors for "for-profit" private sector internship programs are considered below.

Similar To An Education Environment And The Primary Beneficiary Of The Activity

In general, the more an internship program is structured around a classroom or academic experience as opposed to the employer's actual operations, the more likely the internship will be viewed as an extension of the individual's educational experience (this often occurs where a college or university exercises oversight over the internship program and provides educational credit). The more the internship provides the individual with skills that can be used in multiple employment settings, as opposed to skills particular to one employer's operation, the more likely the intern would be viewed as receiving training. Under these circumstances the intern does not perform the routine work of the business on a regular and recurring basis, and the business is not dependent upon the work of the intern. On the other hand, if the interns are engaged in the operations of the employer or are performing productive work (for example, filing, performing other clerical work, or assisting customers), then the fact that they may be receiving some benefits in the form of a new skill or improved work habits will not exclude them from the FLSA's minimum wage and overtime requirements because the employer benefits from the interns' work.

Displacement And Supervision Issues

If an employer uses interns as substitutes for regular workers or to augment its existing workforce during specific time periods, these interns should be paid at least the minimum wage and overtime compensation for hours worked over forty in a workweek. If the employer would have hired additional employees or required existing staff to work additional hours had the interns not performed the work, then the interns will be viewed as employees and entitled compensation under the FLSA. Conversely, if the employer is providing job shadowing opportunities that allow an intern to learn certain functions under the close and constant supervision of regular employees, but the intern performs no or minimal work, the activity is more likely to be viewed as a bona fide education experience. On the other hand, if the intern receives the same level of supervision as the employer's regular work-force, this would suggest an employment relationship, rather than training.

Job Entitlement

The internship should be of a fixed duration, established prior to the outset of the internship. Further, unpaid internships generally should not be used by the employer as a trial period for individuals seeking employment at the conclusion of the internship period. If an intern is placed with the employer for a trial period with the expectation that he or she will then be hired on a permanent basis, that individual generally would be considered an employee under the FLSA.

Where to Obtain Additional Information

This publication is for general information and is not to be considered in the same light as official statements of position contained in the regulations.

For additional information, visit the Wage and Hour Division Website: http://www.wagehour.dol.gov and/or call the toll-free information and helpline, available 8 a.m. to 5 p.m. in your time zone, 1-866-4USWAGE (1-866-487-9243).

The FLSA makes a special exception under certain circumstances for individuals who volunteer to perform services for a state or local government agency and for individuals who volunteer for humanitarian purposes for private non-profit food banks. WHD also recognizes an exception for individuals who volunteer their time, freely and without anticipation of compensation for religious, charitable, civic, or humanitarian purposes to non-profit organizations. Unpaid internships in the public sector and for non-profit charitable organizations, where the intern volunteers without expectation of compensation, are generally permissible. WHD is reviewing the need for additional guidance on internships in the public and non-profit sectors.

About the Author

In a remarkably diverse and successful career encompassing multiple industries and continents, Marv Russell has distinguished himself as an internationalist and a multilingual and multicultural professional; including living and working abroad nearly 10 years with several multi-national companies. His career has spanned government, heavy industry, materials and packaging, pharmaceuticals and healthcare as an executive and as a consultant. He has proven success in the deployment of modern leadership and human capital development techniques. Marv's strong leadership combined with his people and business acumen are key to his ability to coach and create high performing leaders.

Possessing the tenacity to persevere academic life combined with the rigors of Division 1 football, Marv was a successful student-athlete at the University of Notre Dame, played middle linebacker, and was a member of the university's 1973 National Championship Team. He also completed a master's degree at Indiana University and is currently completing PhD studies in Business Technology and Leadership.

Marv is a globally experienced business professional, leadership consultant, motivational speaker, and workshop facilitator who has engaged audiences in both the US and Europe on the topics of leadership, culture and diversity, business ethics and human resource practices. In addition to his corporate experience he has many years experience speaking on leadership topics to Professional Associations, Athletic Organizations, Adolescent Groups, Religious Audiences and Non-Profit Community-Based and Government Organizations. Marv's volunteer board service has included work with YMCA's, Urban Leagues, Youth Services Bureaus and Hospital Systems. These organizations have been inspired by Marv's vision of leadership, workforce development and motivation, multi-cultural business operations, ethics and responsibility, and global and cultural diversity. Through the implementation of cutting edge, passionate programs and workshops, and dynamic message delivery, Marv shares inspirational, humorous, and challenging personal experiences using audience engagement tools and techniques designed to motivate his audience to think and challenge them to succeed in every endeavor.

Marv's first book *Linebacker in the Boardroom: Lessons in Life and Leadership*, published in the fall of 2011, received national attention and was listed as a "new best seller in the leadership and motivation genre". Marv's complete bio and resume can be seen at: http://marvrussell.com/partners/marv-russell/

Marv's *Finding Your Internship* Online Resources

Finding Your Internship links, tips, resources,
coaching support and more can be found at:

www.marvrussell.com/findyourinternimpactzone

http://www.facebook.com/FindYourInternImpactZone

LinkedIn: Join Group "Career Development and Internships"

LinkedIn: Follow Marv Russell

@TheInternZone

@marvrussell

INDEX

CPSIA information can be obtained at www.ICGtesting.com
Printed in the USA
LVOW072353080713

341935LV00003B/14/P

9 781457 520105